STRANGE TRIBE

GENEALOGY OF THE HEMINGWAY FAMILY

Clarence Edmonds Hemingway (1871–1928)
=1896, Grace Hall, (1872–1951)

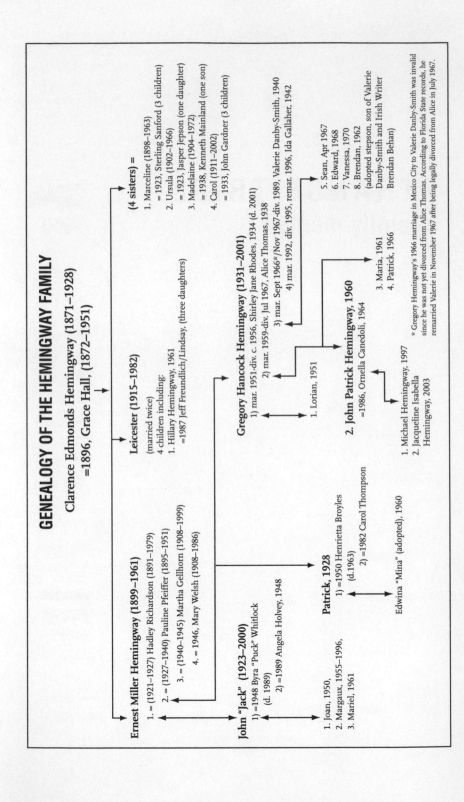

Ernest Miller Hemingway (1899–1961)

1. = (1921–1927) Hadley Richardson (1891–1979)
2. = (1927–1940) Pauline Pfeiffer (1895–1951)
3. = (1940–1945) Martha Gellhorn (1908–1999)
4. = 1946, Mary Welsh (1908–1986)

John "Jack" (1923–2000)
1) =1948 Byra "Puck" Whitlock
(d. 1989)
2) =1989 Angela Holvey, 1948

1. Joan, 1950,
2. Margaux, 1955–1996,
3. Mariel, 1961

Patrick, 1928
1) =1950 Henrietta Broyles
(d.1963)
2) =1982 Carol Thompson

Edwina "Mina" (adopted), 1960

Leicester (1915–1982)

(married twice)
4 children including:
1. Hillary Hemingway, 1961
=1987 Jeff Freundlich/Lindsay, (three daughters)

Gregory Hancock Hemingway (1931–2001)
1) mar. 1951-div. c. 1956, Shirley Jane Rhodes, 1934 (d. 2001)
2) mar. 1959-div. Jul 1967, Alice Thomas, 1938
3) mar. Sept 1966*/Nov 1967-div. 1989, Valerie Danby-Smith, 1940
4) mar. 1992, div. 1995, remar. 1996, Ida Gallaher, 1942

1. Lorian, 1951

2. John Patrick Hemingway, 1960
=1986, Ornella Canedoli, 1964

1. Michael Hemingway, 1997
2. Jacqueline Isabella Hemingway, 2003

3. Maria, 1961
4. Patrick, 1966

5. Sean, Apr 1967
6. Edward, 1968
7. Vanessa, 1970
8. Brendan, 1962
(adopted stepson, son of Valerie
Danby-Smith and Irish Writer
Brendan Behan)

(4 sisters) =

1. Marceline (1898–1963)
   = 1923, Sterling Sanford (3 children)
2. Ursula (1902–1966)
   = 1923, Jasper Jepson (one daughter)
3. Madelaine (1904–1972)
   = 1938, Kenneth Mainland (one son)
4. Carol (1911–2002)
   = 1933, John Gardner (3 children)

* Gregory Hemingway's 1966 marriage in Mexico City to Valerie Danby-Smith was invalid since he was not yet divorced from Alice Thomas. According to Florida State records, he remarried Valerie in November 1967 after being legally divorced from Alice in July 1967.

STRANGE TRIBE
a family memoir

John Hemingway

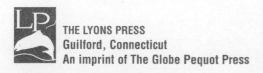

THE LYONS PRESS
Guilford, Connecticut
An imprint of The Globe Pequot Press

To buy books in quantity for corporate use
or incentives, call **(800) 962–0973**
or e-mail **premiums@GlobePequot.com.**

For Greg

The smallest boy was fair and was built like a pocket battleship. He was a copy of Thomas Hudson, physically, reduced in scale and widened and shortened. His skin freckled when it tanned and he had a humorous face and was born being very old. He was a devil too, and deviled both his older brothers, and he had a dark side to him that nobody except Thomas Hudson could ever understand. Neither of them thought about this except that they recognized it in each other and knew that it was bad and the man respected it and understood the boy's having it.

—Ernest Hemingway,
from *Islands in the Stream*

Contents

Acknowledgments

I'd like to thank my agents Jane Dystel and Miriam Goderich for initially reading my book and helping me get it published. Bella gente! Of course, I'd also like to thank my editor, Rob Kirkpatrick, who did a great job in helping me revise Strange Tribe (I was truly lucky to hook up with him). Special thanks to Henry Bisharat and John Lyons for critically reading my book while I was working on it. And to Paolo Piazza, a good friend of mine at the QSS in Milan who helped me out so many times in the early days.

Thanks to Carl Eby whose book was enormously useful in putting together the missing pieces. Molto grazie a mio fratello Patrick, for sending me our father's letters. Thanks to my cousin Hilary Hemingway and her husband Jeff Lindsay for their excellent advice in all things. And special thanks also to Leicester and Doris Hemingway for their generosity and hospitality.

I'm sure, though, that none of this would have been possible without Ornella. She helped me find my agents, she was invaluable as an aid in my research and, most importantly, (and I can't stress this enough) she believed in me, always.

STRANGE TRIBE

Chapter 1

MEMORIES

When I was young, my father was the man who braved the ocean's fury and lived to tell the tale. I saw only his positive side, his generosity and his humor, his kindness, and the way he never failed to make me happy. As a little boy he was the one I looked up to, and it wasn't until much later that I began to realize how he'd inherited more than his fair share of misfortune. He hardly ever talked about his father, and while I knew that my grandfather was a famous writer and a "literary legend," it wasn't something that I was terribly interested in; not when I was young. When I was six, Greg was my Hemingway hero.

By the time I was twelve, I'd slowly started to fill in the missing pieces of his personality—things he'd never revealed to me in conversation, but which were an unavoidable part of his makeup. Just as some biographers have written about Ernest's hatred for his mother, being the son of Gregory H. Hemingway, I couldn't help but pick up on the obsession my dad had with his father. He never wore it on his sleeve, but the conflict between the two, and with his own sexuality, was ever-present. If you hung around him enough, it wasn't too hard to guess at the nature of the numerous beasts that had tormented him for most of his life. He was a manic-depressive, he cross-dressed, and he eventually had a sex change operation. He drank and got into fights, did time in jail, but more than anything else, he missed his father terribly. Missed him and hated him at the same time. Hated him, and blamed himself for Ernest's suicide in 1961.

Of course, it wasn't his fault. My grandfather was in bad shape at the end, and suffering from the combined effects of heavy drinking, memory loss, the various drugs he was taking for his blood pressure and heart condition, and perhaps even from the memory of his own father's suicide. But for my dad, none of that mattered. In the last three years of Ernest's life they weren't communicating much. They'd reached a point after a series of bitter letters where there was nothing more to say, and then it was too late.

The first time I can remember starting to put two and two together was in 1972. I was spending part of the summer with my father in New York City, and one day, when I had nothing better to do, he asked me if I wanted to go out for a walk. I said yes because I thought that maybe we could go to the park or get an ice cream, and also, because you never knew where you might end up with my dad. By chance we passed by a cinema where *The New Centurions* was playing, with George C. Scott, one of my father's favorite actors. My dad asked me if I wanted to see it, and I said, "Sure—why not?"

If there was one thing that Greg liked more than reading it was going to the movies. In the 1960s when my parents were still married he'd often take me with him to see his favorite films. The theaters were usually air-conditioned and in Miami it was a cheap way to beat the heat. For a "double-header" we could go in at two and be out at six in time for dinner. At the age of five I was fast becoming an authority on James Bond and Ian Fleming, having already seen "Dr. No" and "From Russia with Love." I don't know what my mother had to say, or if she approved of me tagging along with my dad, but we were almost always together. At thirty three my father was a man who did more or less what he wanted, and like 007 wasn't afraid of breaking the rules when he had to. He was a serious fan of the man "with a license to kill" and while he didn't have an Aston Martin, he did have a navy blue Jag: an XK 150 with steel spoke tires and beautiful lines that gave it a feeling of power and sensuality. He liked to race it out on the Tamiami Trail late in the afternoon when there was no one around. It was incredibly fast and had a switch on the dash that would put it into a kind of over-drive. Hit it and the needle on the tac would magically swing back over to the far left side of the dial. The torque exploded, my father would smile and the hidden calling of the car was revealed: to provide my dad with that physical, emotional rush that he could never get enough of.

In the theater that afternoon we had our choice of seats. There was hardly anyone there, and I remember thinking that it reminded me of the old days in Miami. He didn't have his Jag anymore but the two of us were alone again in the darkness, staring up at the screen as we had done so many times in the past.

The film was about two patrol cops in LA. Stacey Keach played the rookie, and Scott, the old veteran on the verge of retirement. It was a film that had a neo-realist feel to it, and in the first half there were many scenes that gave you a glimpse of the difficult conditions they worked in. They really were centurions, hired to ride roughshod over the masses. They could only depend on themselves for their survival, and thus, they formed close bonds. In the film Scott becomes a kind of father figure to Keach, and I imagined what my dad must have felt watching it.

He'd lived in Los Angeles in the 1950s, and had spent three years at UCLA. For my father, seeing the wide avenues and low concrete buildings, the bungalows and brown haze hanging over the hills, the summer heat with orange-ozone-colored sunsets would have been familiar. Los Angeles is an unforgiving town, and when Scott retires and decides that he's going to make up for all the lost time and do the things that he should have done before, he gets in touch with the son he'd always been too busy to see when he was a cop. But he discovers that his son doesn't want to talk; that he doesn't have time for his old man. No one does—not his friends or ex-colleagues—and Scott takes it hard. He's alone in his apartment, and he opens a drawer and pulls out a gun, and next to me I heard my dad whisper, "oh, God, no." Then there's a shot of the open blinds on the window with the sunset streaming in and the gun going off, and I looked at my dad, and I could still hear him saying *No, no*, with his head in his hands.

I knew then that he'd never gotten over it.

Chapter 2

BAD BEGINNINGS

I never met my grandmother Pauline. She died nine years before I was born, and judging from the way my father described her, I doubt that I would have seen her much as a child had she lived. The thirteen years of her marriage to Ernest certainly marked one of the most productive periods of his career, but my father had a very negative opinion of her. In an interview in the September 1989 issue of *Fame* magazine, he had this to say about the woman who'd brought him into this world: "I hated the bitch. She was born without the maternal instinct. She never showed any affection towards me. She never kissed me once in my life that I know about. She never held me."[1] In terms of relationships, it was about as fractured as they come, and while Greg would debate the good and the bad of his father all his life, his mother was beyond forgiveness. She had abandoned him, or worse still, had never really claimed him as her son, paying little attention to the formative years of his upbringing. For the most part she'd favored her older son, Patrick, associated as he was with the earlier happy years of her relationship with Ernest. Greg, on the other hand, was raised by the family governess, Ada, and often spent the summer and Christmas holidays with her in her house in up-state New York. Still, I doubt that Patrick's opinion of his mother differed much from my father's. Pauline was buried in the Hollywood Memorial Cemetery, and as a student at UCLA I must have passed by it a thousand times on my way to classes. Still, it wasn't until a friend of mine asked me to spend a couple of hours there with her that I actually visited the place. "We could have a picnic on the grass," she had suggested.

Yet it was the first time I'd ever set foot inside a cemetery, and while I rejected the idea of the picnic, I had to admit that it was peaceful and well kept, and not at all what I'd expected. It was a sunny day, and we had the grounds to ourselves. "Let's sit here," she said, pointing to a grassy area devoid of any markers. For all I know, I could have been sitting on my grandmother's grave.

Years later, I found out from Dr. Ruth Hawkins, the director of the Hemingway-Pfeiffer Museum and Educational Center, that my father and uncle had never bothered to put up a tombstone. They could have afforded one, but clearly felt that Pauline didn't deserve it. "I can't *stand* horrid little children"[2] was how she had once tried to justify her treatment of my father, and when she died, those horrid little children probably had better things to do than worry about tombstones. No sign was left of her passing, nothing that might remind them or anyone else that here lay the remains of the woman who'd once been their mother.

Pauline was a journalist, but unlike Ernest, she'd never had to work for a living. Her father had amassed an enormous fortune in the pharmaceutical industry, and she and her sister Jinny had a freedom from financial worries that my grandfather could only dream of in his early years. They had large trust funds, but also a childless uncle who treated them as if they were his own daughters. The Key West house in which my dad and his brother grew up was in fact a present from my grandmother's uncle, Gus Pfeiffer.

A large, well-ventilated, two-storey French colonial house built in 1851 by a local shipping magnate, it had the only swimming pool on the island, a luxury that my grandmother had added later in an unsuccessful effort to curb her husband's wanderlust. At the time, my grandfather was getting to know the lady who would become his third wife, Martha "Marty" Gellhorn. His stated belief was that if you loved someone, then you should make it official, and for as long as he had the strength to stick to his guns, that's just what he did.

Marty was much more committed to social causes than my grandmother, and meeting her signaled the beginning of the end of my grandfather's Key West period. When Ernest went to Spain to cover the Spanish Civil War, he took Marty with him, not Pauline. Even though my grandmother had expressed her desire to be there, too, Ernest told her that Madrid under a fascist siege was not a proper place for wives. Her place was at home.

The Republican defeat affected him profoundly, and his experiences in Spain and his affair with Marty were masterfully woven into his novel, *For Whom the Bell Tolls*. Published in 1940, the book was an enormous success, and at the height of his fame and in love with a new woman, he was more than ready to ditch Pauline and the financial safety net she had provided. He'd never been comfortable with my grandmother's wealth, and the war only deepened this feeling. He considered it *her* money, and while the financial peace of mind it bought him may have initially supported his literary production, he resented her having it and was not appreciative. Two of his finest stories from that period—"The Short Happy Life of Francis Macomber" and "The Snows of Kilimanjaro"—have as their protagonists men married to rich women. In "The Short Happy Life," Macomber ends up being shot by his wife just when he's started to act like a real man, whereas in the other story, the protagonist, dying of gangrene, accuses his wife of having destroyed his art with her money.

The tour guides at the Key West house had their own way of describing the class warfare that existed between Ernest and Pauline. The story I heard whenever I went down to the Key West house had to do with the pool. According to them, Ernest thought it was a colossal waste of money, and when Pauline surprised him with it (apparently on his way back from one of his trips to Spain with Marty), he angrily threw what he called his last dime into the still-wet cement. As a kid I always looked for that coin whenever I went down there, but could never find it. The truth was that Ernest wasn't at all angry about the pool. In fact, he used it to stay in shape, and the tale of his getting teed off with my grandmother was a bit of invented history that the people who'd bought the house in 1961 had thought of to sell tickets to tourists. Nor were there ever any six-toed cats. The house is full of them now, but according to my father and my uncle Pat, the only animal they ever had as boys was a dog. The cats came later on, in Cuba. Like so many other things you hear about Ernest, it was just part of the legend that had grown up around him.

My dad writes in his memoir that, "Although my early childhood coincided with the Depression, our family had few financial problems. This was partly due to Papa's royalties from *The Sun Also Rises* and *A Farewell to Arms,* but mainly because my mother was rich, a Sloan's Liniment or pain-in-the-ass heiress, as I sometimes thought of her."[3] She had money, and when it came to supporting what she considered a worthy cause, she used it. In addition to the pool, she also had a high wall built around the house and grounds. The idea, as was the case with just about everything she did, was to please Ernest. The wall was there to protect his privacy, or perhaps unconsciously, to keep him in and her competitors out. That my grandfather might have felt the same need is another matter.

Wall or no wall, my father told me that there were endless drifters in Key West in the 1930s, and many of them would come up to the front gate of the house, asking for a handout. My dad usually gave them a dime or a nickel, because, as he put it, "Mother was loaded, and I always had some change in my pockets."

As far as I know, except for the year before his mother's death when he was working as an airplane mechanic, there was never a period in his life when Greg was seriously hurting for money. He either received income or inherited it from his mother or father, or made it on his own as a doctor. Still, anyone who knew my father would not have considered him fortunate. My dad paid his dues, or as the Rolling Stones' song goes, suffered his "fair share of abuse."

Everything about his life was complicated. He was Pauline's second son, and her second caesarean delivery. After his birth on November 12, 1931, the doctors advised against her having another child, saying that her uterus wouldn't be able to handle it. For Ernest this was doubly disappointing. He'd wanted a girl, but so long as he stayed with Pauline he'd be stuck with three sons (my father, Patrick, and John, or "Jack" from Ernest's first marriage) instead of the desired two sons and a daughter. Pauline, as always, wanted desperately to please her husband. So, if Ernest was upset, then so was she.

While technically Greg was her offspring, Pauline had no maternal instinct or desire to deal with toddlers. Combined with the fact that Greg's gender was not what her husband had ordered, Pauline put this baby boy at the very end of her list of priorities. So Greg became the problem of Ada Stern, their governess, an alcoholic who was cruelly manipulative. My uncle Patrick once said that as a three-year-old, he had a very clear idea of who his mother was. For Greg that was definitely not the case. He was terrified of losing Ada, because she was all he had. Unfortunately, as a surrogate mom, Ada had many rules that my father had to obey, and whenever he'd break one, as little boys are wont to do, she'd threaten to leave. It was a nasty joke to play on a three-year-old, and my father would panic and start to scream, "Don't leave me—please don't leave me!" and she'd shout back at him, "All right, I'll stay, you little shitsky. But if you misbehave one more time . . ."[4] And so it would go.

Whenever Ernest and Pauline planned one of their adventurous trips to Europe or Africa, my father stayed with Ada. Patrick might go with them or be sent to his maternal grandparents in Piggott, Arkansas, as an alternative, but Greg almost always went with Ada to her house in upstate New York. On one of the few occasions when Greg was left with his mother and Ada was away with Patrick, Pauline complained that her youngest son had turned into "the lousiest type of mama's boy." He missed his governess and was always clinging to Pauline and crying out whenever he lost sight of her. Intolerant of bawling kids, she regretted anew the fact that he hadn't turned out to be the little girl that she'd wanted so badly.[5]

Sometimes I try to imagine the kind of man my father might have been had his mother taken more than a passing interest in his upbringing. I like to dream about how everything could have been different, and how I wouldn't have lost so much time trying to piece together the puzzle of his crazy existence. There never would have been a need to distance myself, moving to Europe to find my own space and a different perspective. Nor would there have been that ten-year interruption (from 1987 to 1997) when the two of us severed all communication. He probably wouldn't have been able to avoid his manic depression, seeing as how both Ernest and Ernest's father, Clarence, had also suffered from it, but the stress that Greg had to deal with during his childhood didn't help. He drank heavily to cope with his unhappy memories, and alcohol is often a trigger of this disease. Just a little extra attention from his mother might have gone a long way. Greg certainly wouldn't have been as insecure, and he would have been better prepared to deal with the weight of such a famous family name. He'd have been a happier man, and perhaps less troubled by his own sexuality. No one would have complained about the daughter that wasn't, and his mother would have loved him for the bright little boy that he was. And perhaps, had his mother been there for him, the "unnaturally close relationship" with his father, as he put it, wouldn't have been so overwhelmingly important.

I can understand what he must have gone through, because my own mother is schizophrenic, and a close relationship with her was a luxury I never had. As a kid I remember that she was always on the verge of, or recovering from, a nervous break-down, drinking and telling us, as we traipsed from one motel to another, that we were "much more important than the Kennedys." At one point, just before the three of us went to live with our great-uncle Leicester, she'd even come up with the odd-ball solution of handing my brother Patrick, my sister Maria, and myself over to the Catholic Church. She wanted to become a nun and figured that the Church would meet her halfway. I knew that she was becoming more religious, but I had no idea what was in store for us. She'd been shopping religions for about six months, and before settling on the Catholics, she'd taken the Baptists and the Congregationalists for a test drive. At the age of twelve, I was forced to endure Sunday School classes and the ecstatic ministers half-drowning the faithful in large tanks of water because, when either of your parents tell you to do something at that age, you either grin and bear it, or you run away from home, which for me wasn't an option. Where would I have gone? And what would have happened to my brother and sister? I felt responsible for them and knew that I couldn't leave them alone with my mother.

When my mother broke the news to me of her intentions, I remember pointing out to her that she couldn't become a nun, since everyone knew nuns were virgins, and she'd already had three kids. She said that it wasn't a problem—the Pope could make an exception—and that soon, the three of us would be living with the priests because she had decided to live in a nunnery. I tried to put it down as just another of my mom's phases, but when she told me a few days later that a priest wanted to talk to me, I realized that she was being serious after all. It was certainly one of the more difficult periods of my life. My mother was insane, and while perhaps I'd always suspected it, at least she was our mother and she wanted us to live with her. But when she said that we could go camp out at the church, something just buckled inside of me. It was bad enough when my parents had gotten divorced, but this was worse. She was basically saying, "*ciao*—get out of my life." Many years would pass before I was able to come to terms with the emotional damage of her rejection, which was certainly something akin to what my father had to go through with Pauline.

The priest, of course, had no intention of letting my mom dump three kids on the Church. He confirmed the fact that nuns were indeed virgins, and suggested that my mother needed help. Was there anyone in the family who we could stay with? I told him about Great-Uncle Leicester, Ernest's younger brother, who was living in Miami Beach with his family at the time. The next day, Les and his wife Doris appeared at our apartment to take us away.

Needless to say, with a mother as unstable and remote as mine, I tended to put all my emotional eggs in my father's basket. My dad had his own problems, but you never got the feeling that there was a wall between the two of you as you did with my mom. While my mother grew ever more pious and cloistered in her affections, although she never did become a nun, my dad was a person I could count on. If my mother was weak, my father was strong. He was an MD, and when I grew up, I wanted to be a doctor, too. I wanted to do everything he did, and even if he lived in New York with his new family, I knew that he still loved me very much, and that someday we'd be together again. It was a clear case of out-and-out hero worship—but what's a young boy to do? Just as my father had turned to his father, I felt that there was no one else I could depend on, if not Greg.

Chapter 3

GETTING TO KNOW HIM

Unfortunately, my father needed a helping hand as much as I did. He didn't function well on his own, and when he was alone, it showed. The first time I came face-to-face with his periodic disintegration was in 1985. I was twenty-four, and had gone out to Missoula, Montana, to spend some time with him, not too long after his third wife had filed for divorce. I'd been in Italy for a year, and when I got back to the States in June, with less than two dollars in my pocket, I needed somewhere to stay. I remember calling him collect from a public pay phone in Buffalo. Luckily for me, he was home. We hadn't been in touch since Christmas when I'd mailed him a postcard, and he was very surprised to discover that I was stateside. Generous as ever, he immediately offered to wire me some money for a bus ticket, telling me that I could hang out with him for as long as I wanted, or at least until I decided what my next move would be.

So I caught the first bus out of the city heading west. I traveled day and night for over sixty hours, and on the last day when the bus stopped in Butte, Montana, for dinner, I tried calling him several times, but without any luck. I spent the hour and a half before the bus arrived in Missoula thinking that he'd probably be there waiting for me, but he wasn't. At the station I tried calling his apartment, but again, no one answered. At that point I started to think that he'd either changed his mind about inviting me, or had completely forgotten that I was coming, which was also quite possible.

Spending the night in the bus station was not an option. The guy who worked behind the counter was turning off all the lights and getting ready to go home. I had to leave. He told me there was an all-night truck-stop café near the highway, so I walked over to it. I kept calling my dad's apartment from a pay phone there until about two in the morning, when I gave up and found a place out in a field where I managed to sleep.

As soon as it was light I went back to the truck stop and dialed his number again. This time he answered and whispered in a sleepy voice, "Fuck."

"It's me," I said. "John!" But he hung up. I redialed.

This time, he asked where I was. In Missoula, I told him, and emerging from his early-morning grogginess, he vaguely remembered that he was supposed to have met me at the bus station. "Really am sorry about last night," he said.

"It's still okay if I come, right?"

"Of course it is, but I can't come pick you up now. I gotta get off to this job, and I'm already late." It was a strange excuse, considering that I was his son who'd traveled thousands of miles to see him, but at the time I was just so happy to have connected with him that I didn't give it much thought. After he explained to me where the house was, we said good-bye and I started walking.

His apartment was in a new two-storey building, which looked like a motel, located on the other side of town near a stream. There was a swimming pool, and a few cars in the parking lot. My dad had left the key under the doormat. When I opened the door, the first thing that hit me was the smell: a mixture of mold and stale beer, the kind of early-warning signal that should have told me, even before I switched on the lights and could see the chaos, that here was a man in need of help. I was greeted by a maid's nightmare. It was a mess of mammoth proportions, with the remains of several TV dinners piled up all over the living room and the kitchen, next to medical texts and journals, and on the stairs that led to the second floor. The kitchen sink was filled with grimy plastic forks and knives and beer bottles, and the drain was surrounded by thick grease which looked a bit like Cheez Whiz mixed with spaghetti.

The dark-green wall-to-wall carpeting had not been cleaned for months. It was engrained with crumbs of corn and rice, hamburger patties and ketchup, french fries, and other substances. It would have taken me at least a week to clean up if I'd kept at it, and was lucky enough to find an industrial-strength cleaner that could have removed all the stains. Upstairs there was a water bed, a bathroom, and a balcony overlooking the tree-lined stream. T-shirts were scattered on the floor, and a pair of khaki slacks was slung over a pile of newspapers. He had a long-sleeved shirt in the closet and a pair of tennis shoes and shorts. And that was it.

So here was the son of Ernest Hemingway, I thought, an MD, living like a hermit and wearing his pants and shoes until they fell apart, or became so stained that he just threw them away. How could anyone live in such filth? And yet it didn't seem to bother him. In fact, Greg was so oblivious to it, so deep in his depression, that he was far beyond worrying about his environment, or about what others might think. I was stunned, and I'm sure that my emotional reaction had much to do with the mental picture I had of my father. How did he get from the essentially positive childhood memories I had of him, to this? I knew that he was a manic-depressive, but hearing about it was one thing—seeing it was another. It was a definite wake-up call, a sign that I hadn't connected all the dots. There was a good deal that I didn't understand about my dad.

It wasn't the first time he'd let himself go. When his relationship with his first wife, Shirley "Jane" Rhodes, started to fall apart during an African safari in Tanzania in 1955, he took it badly. He'd had an affair with the daughter of a neighboring plantation owner, and that, combined with his cross-dressing, had convinced his wife it was time to leave. Jane went back to her sister's house in Arkansas with their daughter, my older sister Lorian. Greg tried to salvage the situation and begged his wife to forgive him. He followed her back to the States, but she didn't want to hear his apologies. She'd had enough. My father started to drink heavily, and was later arrested for disturbing the peace in Pine Bluff. About a year after that, when Jane had remarried, he visited them again on his way back from another trip to Africa. The shirt and trousers that he was wearing, basically all that he had, were torn and dirty, and he looked very thin and depressed. Lorian's stepfather gave Greg some of his clothes, but said that Greg had lost so much weight, he couldn't find a belt that fit him. Again Greg asked his ex-wife if she'd come back with him, and again she said no, and he left.

He married my mother, Alice Thomas, in 1959. They had been introduced to each other by a mutual friend when they were both studying at the University of Miami. My mother was tolerant of my dad's cross-dressing, but not of his affairs. In his memoir, in which strangely enough his second wife and family are never mentioned, Greg says that he met the woman who would replace my mother in Idaho at my grandfather's funeral. Valerie Danby Smith had been one of Ernest's secretaries, and by March of 1966, when my brother Patrick was born, she and Greg were very much an item.

About six months before my parents divorced in 1967, he sometimes came over to our house in Coconut Grove, Miami, to talk to my mother and to see his kids. He was already living with Valerie, who was pregnant with their first son, Sean. Yet, apparently he was having second thoughts about his new companion, or feeling guilty about what he'd done, and wondered if my mother would have him back. I don't know what my mother answered, but I do remember Valerie following him up to our doorstep one day and arguing with my mom. It was a classic battle between two women over a man. Valerie had come to retrieve what she considered hers, and my mother was incensed, telling her that she had no right to be there, and threatening to call the police if she didn't leave. I can't remember if my father went outside to calm them down or not. But I'm sure that even if he ended up taking a few punches from either my mom or Valerie, he didn't mind being the center of attention. For Greg it was always better to be fought over than dumped.

The hardest thing for him was letting go, even if he was the one at fault. His childhood fear of being abandoned had never left him. He married four times, and with each divorce, he relived, almost ritualistically, the nightmare of not having anyone to depend on. He became depressed, let himself go, and usually came out of it after a series of electroshock treatments. It was the pattern that his life followed, with the exception, perhaps, of the last time he tried to leave a wife.

Ernest was also married four times, and seemed to have had as much of a problem dealing with women as my father did. He was the world's most masculine writer, an artist whose image was that of a hard-drinking action man, obsessed with courage, the loss of freedom, and death. Yet any literary scholar would be hard-pressed to find a man more dependent on the opposite sex. Excluding his period in Italy during the First World War, and just before he married Hadley Richardson in 1921, he never lived alone. There was always a woman around to take care of him. Like my father, he couldn't do without a companion. He was forever in search of an equilibrium between the male and female side of his character. Jung refers to these two sides as the *animus/anima* that exists within each of us. To become a balanced man requires understanding and accepting the feminine part of one's character. Problems arise when one side prevails over the other. Ernest must have sensed the danger, and as a result, gender was a strong current throughout his work.

But if my grandfather experimented with gender in his writing, my father took it to another level. His was the physical manifestation of EMH's fascination with androgyny. They were two sides of the same coin, a similarity that only they would recognize.

Chapter 4

MY PARENTS: THE ODD COUPLE

The Italians have a saying for the odd couples in life: *Dio li fa e poi li accoppia*—,God makes them and then brings them together. It's an ironic way of explaining the seemingly inexplicable. My father, who wanted to become a woman; and my mother, who hated men and yet loved my father; it was a marriage made in heaven. When I was a teenager I sometimes wondered how I could be the product of these two and not end up having their problems. I thought it amazing that I was "normal," coming as I did from the double whammy of manic depression and schizophrenia. I didn't know that these illnesses, while hereditary, could skip a generation, or fade out of the gene pool entirely. I just saw my mother and father as they were (and as I wasn't), and thought that I'd been extremely lucky.

In the beginning there was nothing that hinted at my mother's future troubles; quite the contrary. As the eldest daughter of John G. Thomas Sr. and Caroline Whitmore, she was a straight-A student with a photographic memory who excelled at everything she did. She loved the sea, and during her senior year in high school, she sailed a twelve-meter ketch from Miami to Havana with a group of sea scouts. Her family was normal enough, solidly middle-class. My maternal grandfather was a lawyer, and for many years the city attorney for Coral Gables. He was a prominent Miami Republican, and a good friend of Richard Nixon and Bebe Rebozo. They were drinking buddies, and spent numerous afternoons fishing out on the Gulf Stream. The three of them would pack a boat with bait and beer, and once even the Secret Service couldn't find them. Two agents showed up at the house asking my grandmother if she knew where the vice president was.

When I lived in Miami, my grandfather was a constant presence in my life. My parents were always taking us over to their small, rose-colored house. John G. Thomas was a tall, lanky Kentuckian from Louisville, with deep blue eyes and a voice and presence which according to my father were absolutely mesmerizing. "He could go into a courtroom and rip apart the defendant's case before the guy ever knew what had hit him. He was that good," my father told me. There was a strong bond between the two, and my dad may have looked up to him as the kind of man he would have liked to have been, or the understanding father that at the time he didn't have. I remember that when I was going to UCLA, Greg said that I should study law instead of history. He told me that he regretted having pursued a career in medicine, and that a legal mind like my grandfather's was a powerful tool. In a phone conversation I had with Greg a few months before he died, he said that he thought about John Thomas every day, and that he missed him terribly. Certainly it was easier for him to relate to my mother's father than it had been with Ernest in the last years. But it was also true that here were the two men he cared about most, both of my grandfathers—brilliant, and yet fragile personalities.

My grandmother was from an old Connecticut family that went as far back as the 1600s, and perhaps even as far as the

Mayflower. She was proud of this heritage, and once showed me an official pedigree that she'd been given with all the names of ancestors whose DNA she carried. About two or three years after she retired as a schoolteacher, she inherited a sizeable sum of money from her great-uncle. I don't know exactly how much it was, but it was enough to turn her life around. I remember that she bought everyone new cars, and that soon thereafter she separated from her husband. She started taking world cruises, remarried a few times, became a widow once, and eventually settled down in Santa Barbara, where she bought a lot of property and hobnobbed with the Reagan-era elite.

She and my mother had a tense relationship. They didn't have much in common, and I'm sure that my mother put up with her because she knew that someday she stood to inherit, and didn't want to burn her bridges. Unfortunately, she never did inherit anything. My grandmother died in 1995, in an old-age home. In the last years of her life, the people who had been managing her estate made a number of bad investments and lost almost everything she had.

Clearly, if my mother resembled anyone, it was her father—more pensive, and less concerned with material things. Although, to be honest, it's hard for me to say just who the real Alice is. As a schizophrenic, much of her is hidden. Sometimes she's completely cut off from the outside world, lost in her voices and paranoia. Then, at other times, she's the most talkative, personable woman imaginable. I don't know what triggers the shutdowns, but you feel a definite mask—a barrier between yourself and whatever she's hiding behind.

According to her brother, John, the biggest change in her personality came about when she met Greg. My mother was always different, he said, an intellectual; but nothing out of the ordinary. So long as she was surrounded by normal people, everything was okay.

"The problem comes when you get two people like Greg and Alice and put 'em together," John said. "Something clicks, and they realize that they're not just a species of one. I'm like you and you're like me, they must have thought. Their bohemian tendencies could run amok, and it was cool."

One of the earliest pictures that I have of my mother is from her honeymoon trip to Paris. She's standing on the observation deck of the Eiffel Tower. She was very young, about twenty, and her nose still had that long Thomas look to it. Another photo that dates back to the day she brought me home from the hospital for the first time is altogether different. She's sitting in a white VW Bug, holding me when I couldn't have been more than a week old, and her nose is looking a lot shorter, more like Pauline Pfeiffer's. My mother told me that it was Greg who'd suggested she get the nose job. She also had a skin peel to remove her freckles, which was not the most intelligent thing to do for someone who lived in Miami. Her skin would never be as protective as it had been before the operation, and that meant having an ever-ready supply of sunscreen in the boiling heat of Southern Florida. I don't know if it was my dad's idea, but after the skin peel and the nose job, the facial similarities between Alice and my grandmother Pauline were striking.

About eleven months after the photo of "Baby John in the VW Bug" was taken, my grandfather Ernest killed himself. Obviously, I was too young to remember anything of his suicide, the funeral, or the media coverage that the world devoted to his passing. My father wrote in his memoir that he felt relief when Ernest died, as if a great weight had been removed; never again would he have to worry about hurting his father.

While initially both he and his brothers had effectively been cut out of the will, Mary was eventually persuaded to include them. My father did some research into U.S. copyright laws, which proved that as sons, they could not be disinherited. With the money that he then started receiving from his father's estate, Greg was able to concentrate on his medical studies and complete his degree in 1964.

Throughout his life, as had been the case with his father, personal hygiene was more a matter of opinion than necessity, and while a student he was no different. He could go for weeks without washing, and my mother would have to tell him to take a bath first before they made love. He hardly ever wore socks, and in his senior year his classmates decided to buy him a pair as a graduation present.

The first house that I can remember living in was on Mary Street in Coconut Grove. A small, white, two-bedroom place, it was typical of the old-style houses built to withstand hurricanes, with an enormous backyard where I played in the afternoons after school, and where my father kept his boat on a trailer. On their own, my parents weren't much when it came to keeping anything clean. Tidying up was for other people to do, and they had a maid to serve this purpose. Rose was an enormous black woman who took care of the house—and my sister Maria and me—when my parents weren't around, which was fairly often. Rose usually slept at our house when my parents were out of town. But one weekend we stayed with Rose and her family in a very run-down section of the city. I remember that the street where they lived was unpaved. In front of the house there was a rusting, wheel-less Chevy propped up on concrete blocks, and Maria and I were the only two white kids in the neighborhood. Rose's family was poor, but they were very kind, and I was sad when she found another job and stopped working for our family.

It was during this period that things started to fall apart for my parents. They argued a lot, and my father was probably already preparing for the jump that would set him up with the woman who would replace my mother. In the fall of 1965 we moved to Boston. My father had decided to do a residency in internal medicine at Massachusetts General Hospital. I was enrolled in a local kindergarten, and we rented a two-storey redbrick house on a hill. We spent one winter there, so I got to see what snow was like for the first time in my life. Just before we moved, my mother discovered she was pregnant. On March 31, 1966, my brother Patrick was born.

Patrick's birth didn't seem to help my parents' problems much. They continued to argue, and in the summer my mother took the three of us back to Miami. After they divorced in 1967, my mother moved us around a lot. In her schizophrenic paranoia, the neighbors were always "out to get us," and as a result, we went from Kendall to South Miami to Coconut Grove, staying in the large apartment complexes that were springing up all over the southland in the late 1960s. The important thing for my mom was that the apartment be new—that it didn't have a history. As she bounced us around from one place to the next, the virgin quality of the housing she found probably helped her maintain the illusion of being just one step ahead of the "crazies" who wouldn't let her "live in peace." Needless to say, always having to move from one apartment complex to another was not my ideal. Long-term friendships were virtually impossible. As soon as I was settled into a school and had found my own crowd, *Boom!* My mother would be off on another one of her wild goose chases.

In the years after my parents' divorce, I can remember two of my mother's nervous breakdowns. The first was in 1970. I was spending the summer with my father in New York City, and instead of going back to Miami, both Patrick and Maria were brought up to New York to join us. Greg had found them in the pigsty that passed for my mom's apartment. I don't know where

Alice was, or how my father found out that my brother and sister had been abandoned. A police officer or a social worker must have called him. I remember seeing my mom one afternoon at the end of August. She'd taken a bus up from Richmond where she'd moved, and perhaps thought that Greg would get back together with her again, finance a new lifestyle or a wardrobe or something. She was always full of ideas. Later on, I found out that she'd been hospitalized and had had electroshock treatments.

With Maria and Patrick I spent my fourth grade year living in New York with Greg and Val. Maria and I went to PS[6], a public school on 81st Street, while Val's son Brendan was going to St. David's, a private Catholic school. It was my first experience in a public school, and while I can't remember if I learned much, I did make a few good friends. Brendan was a year younger than me, and while for the most part we got along, there was certainly a bit of rivalry of the kind you'd expect between siblings. What didn't help matters was the boxing that Greg and Valerie condoned, if not encouraged, between the two of us. My father had a fixation with boxing, and he bought each of us a pair of gloves and then "staged" matches where we were told to go at it. At the time I was a lot more aggressive than Brendan, and a number of times I really lit into him. What surprised me was not so much my father's attitude, but Valerie's. I think she believed that by enduring all my punches, her eldest son would become tougher in some way. I can even remember her almost shouting to Brendan to "fight back."

The next summer Maria and Patrick were sent down to live with Alice in Miami. By then, Alice had decided she was ready to be a mother again. I thought that I'd be spending another year at PS 6, but instead, at the last minute, I was told that arrangements had been made for me to attend Rumsey Hall, a boarding school in Connecticut. It had always been fairly clear to me that Valerie resented the extra burden of Greg's other kids. She had her own family, and probably felt that she had done more than her fair share to help us out. For my part, I can't say that I was overly upset at finally being out of her house. I understood intuitively that I would never be a part of her family, and so I was determined to make the best of my new situation.

We all had to write letters home at least once a week, and I may have even received a phone call or two from my father, but essentially, I was on my own. The one weekend that I didn't spend at the school was at a friend's house. I didn't ask my father for anything while I was at Rumsey Hall, and when the black loafers that I was wearing had worn so thin that there was a hole in the sole, I stuck pieces of cardboard in the bottoms to try to keep my feet from getting wet. I think that at the end of the school year, all my socks had to be thrown out. I wanted a new pair of shoes, and I'm sure that my father would have bought me several had I asked, but I was afraid to let them know I needed anything. According to my shell-shocked logic, that would have been a sign of weakness, and I was not about to let them see me weak. In June, when my father finally saw my polished but worn out shoes, he asked me why I hadn't said anything. I made up some excuse about not wanting to bother him, or being too busy. I never told him the truth.

That summer vacation I was sent down to Miami. My mom had another apartment in the Kendall area, and seemed happy enough. She enrolled me in a sailing camp at the Miami Yacht Club, and for four weeks I learned about lines and bows, starboards and sterns, luffing and what to do when the wind dies down and you're out in the middle of the bay with nowhere to go. It was fun, and I realized that while I liked my new school, I liked being with my mother (when she was okay) even more.

I was supposed to go back to Rumsey Hall in September, and I did pack my bags and get on the plane. But by the time I got to New York and saw my father, I was crying. I told him that I wanted to live with my mother, and for Greg, this was enough. While he'd never had much of a family life as a boy, as an adult he tried a number of times to re-create this ideal. He'd always regretted the fact that his mother had virtually ignored him as a child, and although he had legal custody of me, he certainly wasn't about to keep me from Alice.

And so a few days later I was back on a plane, en route to Miami. I spent another year and a half with my mother before her next nervous breakdown. More schools, more apartments, "new beginnings" that would never be enough to keep her safe from the imaginary stalkers of her paranoia. It was her religious period, the one where she tried to give us away to the Catholic Church. Her schizophrenic voices were talking to her big-time, and she would spend hours sitting on the couch or her bed, saying nothing, or laughing suddenly for no apparent reason. When I'd ask her what was so funny, she'd tell me, "Oh, they say the funniest things, you know."

"No, I don't," I'd tell her, furious and frustrated in the extreme because I could see her getting worse, and there wasn't anything I could do about it—or anyone, I felt, I could call for help. I just had to tough it out, taking care of my brother and sister and hoping that sooner or later, she'd come to her senses.

The chemical imbalances that had been genetically hardwired into my mother's brain were such that if she didn't take her medication, she would crash. Like my father, she had a need for speed. She was in love with the "creativity" of her voices, and they were, at the same time, her source of entertainment and her protection from the outside world. But they couldn't protect her from her drinking. One morning I saw her car weaving slowly into the parking lot after a night spent God only knows where. As her voices became stronger, her trips to the liquor store were a daily occurrence. I thought it amazing that she hadn't totaled the yellow VW Squareback that my grandmother had given her. Her bedroom was littered with empty beer cans and bottles of Jim Beam, and I had this horrible feeling that she was going to die in an accident. Luckily for her, she was arrested a few days after Christmas. She spent a weekend in jail, and her license was suspended for three months.

After that it was all downhill. She kept drinking and talking to her voices and her priest, eventually breaking the news to me that the Church would take care of us for a while. It was one of those turning points in your life that nothing can prepare you for. One day I was living with my family, and the next I wasn't. The young priest, who I knew from catechism classes, found my great-uncle Leicester in the phone book, gave him a call, and that was the end of my early period with Alice.

Chapter 5

IF THE SHOE FITS

When my father was about twelve years old, Ernest walked in on him one day as he was trying on a pair of his mother's nylons. Ernest didn't say anything, but my dad could tell that he was shocked. He had a look on his face

of such devastation and horror and just, yuck . . . Oh, my God! A couple of weeks later he said to me, "Gigi, we come from a strange tribe, you and I." [Gigi, pronounced "Giggy," was Ernest's nickname for Greg.] To someone who is wearing his mother's stockings almost every day, this wasn't all that reassuring. I'm not sure if seeing a therapist would have done me any good, but we should have tried it. Instead of all this elliptical shit about the strange tribe, I probably should have seen somebody about this when I was young. But now when I look back on it—maybe I'm reading more into it than is there—the look of horror on his face may not just have been "What's wrong with my boy?" Maybe it was "What's wrong with the family? My God! Is he doing this too?" Because he was just too masculine to believe."[6]

Growing up, I often wondered the same thing. What was the connection between my father and my grandfather? Was Greg's cross-dressing something casual that he'd picked up along the way, like a hobby or an acquired taste for scotch or grappa, or was there a familial or genetic factor at play? When I asked my dad what he got out of it, he told me that dressing up as a woman helped him deal with stress. As a conscious reason, this seemed believable enough, and I remember thinking, perhaps about a year after I was with him in Missoula, that everyone had different ways of coping. Some took to alcohol or drugs, while others found relief in religion or work or family. My father was different; he bought nylons.

The first time I heard about his passion for cross-dressing was in 1982, when I went to his house in Bozeman, Montana, for a week during the summer. He was still married to Valerie, and had finally convinced her to leave Manhattan and move out to the Big Sky State. Unfortunately, he didn't work in Bozeman. He was the sole doctor in a county hospital way out in Jordan, on the other side of the state. He was commuting the 700 miles round-trip once every two weeks to be with his wife and her kids. It was a long haul, and he said that he would have much preferred to work in Bozeman, but he hadn't been able to find a job there. Jordan was a small town with a few stores and a couple of bars, and there wasn't much to do there if you didn't like rural living. He was sleeping in a trailer parked out behind the hospital. It was a solitary life, but being out of town and away from his wife had its advantages.

Valerie didn't approve of her husband's cross-dressing, and went so far as to state in an interview, before her memoir was published, that when he was with her, he was "normal." He may have acted up with his previous wives, and he had his sex-change surgery after their relationship ended, but for as long as they were married, Greg was just a regular guy. "I never, ever saw him crossed-dressed," she said.[7] My father, however, was much more consistent, and there was never any break in his tendencies. His interest in "the other half of the sky" was lifelong, and it was one of my brothers who enlightened me to this fact. Valerie and my dad were out of town when I was visiting in 1982, and I had the keys to Greg's white Subaru. One day, when we were getting ready to go into Bozeman to see a movie, I opened up the trunk of the car and found some lipstick.

"Is this your mom's?" I asked.

"It's Pa's," my brother answered.

"Dad's?"

"Sure," he said nonchalantly. "He dresses up as a woman. You didn't know?" And I told him that I didn't, and he said that that wasn't all. He also shaved his legs and wore wigs when he was in Jordan.

"Plus," he added, "he doesn't like beards."

"He doesn't?"

"No."

I thought it was all pretty strange, but then, there were many things about my father which weren't conventional. Admittedly, I hadn't seen him looking like a woman, and I was only hearing about it secondhand, but I can't say that it changed the opinion I had of him. I still loved him and thought of him as my father, albeit somewhat eccentric. When I got back to Los Angeles I told my mother about it, but she wasn't impressed.

"Oh, that!" she said. "He used to do that when I was married to him." It was the big family secret, which wasn't, it seemed, very secret at all.

While Ernest certainly didn't approve of his son dressing up in drag, and may have secretly fretted over the generational genetic implications of this behavior, had he lived long enough, he certainly would have admired Greg's grace under pressure. About a year after my visit to Bozeman, my dad grew tired of dressing up for himself in the trailer parked behind the hospital where he worked, and started to go into the cowboy bars in Jordan as Gloria or Valerie, or one of the other female names he'd use. When I heard about it two years later from a judge in Missoula, who'd read the police files on Greg, I couldn't help but admire the sheer boldness of his act. Anyone could walk into a club in LA or New York wearing fishnet stockings and stilettos and order a beer, but for him to do that in a cowboy bar out in the-middle-of-nowhere, Montana—now *that* was a statement.

"You know what's great about this state?"—he once asked me as we were driving back from Flathead Lake to Missoula—"The freedom. You really can do whatever you want here." I wasn't so sure if that was true, but there did seem to be room for everybody. From the far-rightist militias and the hippies, to the artists, the ranchers, and Gregory H. Hemingway, MD, no one was deemed too extreme.

The day I'd arrived in Missoula in 1985 and discovered the chaos of my father's apartment, I also went to his bank to cash the check that he'd left for me on the kitchen table. It was in the center of town, and that morning there was only one teller behind the counter. When it was my turn, I gave her the check and some ID. She looked at me and asked, "Are you his son?" I told her that I was, and that I was visiting. She was an attractive young woman in her twenties, with long black hair and pretty brown eyes.

"I know Dr. Hemingway lives alone," she said, "so he must be happy to see you."

"It's good to be here," I told her as she counted out the $50 in fives.

"He's really a charming man."

"Charming?"

"Very intelligent and sweet, but . . . I . . . "

"Come again?"

"And handsome too, and, well—" And here she seemed to be at a loss for words. "You know how he is . . ."

"Of course."

"Different," she said, and it was at this point that I was sure he'd tried to put the moves on her, either by asking her out or sending her flowers, or maybe even proposing. Something had happened, and it didn't surprise me. While he criticized Ernest for being hypermasculine, he was hardly a shy novice when it came to courting the opposite sex. Like anyone else, he didn't always get what he wanted, but his combination of intelligence, humor, and energy was certainly captivating. Women liked him, and he liked women. Even after his sex-change surgery, he never expressed an interest in men. He was straight, but with a chaser—expressing both halves of his personality, each as fundamental to his character as the other.

My first vision of him in drag was on July 1, 1985. I remember the date because it was Canada Day, and I was in his apartment watching TV, and the Canadian ambassador was being interviewed on the *Today* show. It was about nine o'clock, and I was waiting to see if my father would show up before I went out to get something to eat. He hadn't come home after work the night before, and I was curious about what had happened to him. The job that he had at the state prison in Deer Lodge wasn't very interesting, but it was a job, and not too far from *Missoula*. A week and a half had passed since my conversation with the bank teller, and I was getting used to life with Greg. In the mornings he'd go off to the prison, and I'd spend the day walking around town, or reading a book in the park on the other side of the creek next to his apartment block. When he came home we usually went out to a restaurant or cafeteria for dinner. Greg liked to eat out, and neither of us was much of a cook.

Things were looking up, I thought. The situation was stable, and he'd even offered to pay for my master's degree at the local university. He told me that my BA in history wouldn't get me anywhere in life, and that I had to think ahead. Obviously he wanted someone to stay with him, to take care of him, but I wasn't too hot on the idea of going back to school. I'd had enough of higher education. At the same time, I didn't want to say no and rub him the wrong way, especially when I was thinking of inviting my girlfriend Ornella down from Ontario. His apartment was certainly big enough, and the town was pretty. I met Ornella on a tram coming home from work one evening in Milan. Her father was an Italian and her mother French-Canadian. She was born in Northern Ontario but had lived in Italy since she was fifteen and when I met her she'd just turned twenty.

Missoula is a Native American word, meaning "a place between two rivers." It lies on a plain at the far end of a pass between low-lying mountains, and I was sure Ornella would like it. When my father wasn't working, we could take trips up to Glacier, or over into Idaho to go rafting on the Snake River.

Like Ernest, my dad was a great fan of the American West. He'd spent a lot of time in Montana and Idaho as a boy, and an entire chapter of his memoir is dedicated to the summer and fall of 1940 when he and his brothers fished and hunted with their father in Sun Valley. It was perhaps one of the happiest times of his life, and reading his book, I could well understand the need he had to share these experiences with his children. That's why he'd sent me out to Ketchum for the first time in 1970, to stay with his brother, Jack—Ernest and Hadley's son—who was a well-known conservationist and outdoorsman. Jack spoke fluent French and had worked as a spy for the OSS (now the CIA) during World War II. He was dropped behind enemy lines in occupied France, captured, and interned in a POW camp in Germany.

I was duly impressed by the scars he'd received from a German machine gun as he parachuted down, caused when part of the muscle tissue in his upper arm had been removed. When I asked him if he'd ever met the soldier who'd shot him, Jack replied, "Never got a chance to ask him his name." He said this with a smile, while patting me on the back.

Staying with my uncle and getting a taste for the kind of life that he'd lived was supposedly what being a Hemingway was all about—the hunting and the fishing and the war stories. However, the morning I first saw my father dressed in drag was a stark departure from this kind of experience. The man who briefly stuck his head into the apartment that morning was dressed more for a night out on the town than a weekend of hunting or fishing. Greg was wearing a blond wig, a knee-length, cream-colored sequined dress, and matching high-heeled shoes. His cherry-red lipstick was smudged, and he reminded me of a four-year-old who's decided to play with his mother's cosmetics. He looked surprised, or at least pretended to be. If he'd really wanted to keep it a secret, there were a number of places where he could have changed before coming home.

Even if his entrance wasn't staged, on a subconscious level, it seemed in part to be a reenactment of the morning when Ernest had walked in on him as a boy. The only difference was that this time, it was the father in drag walking in on the son, dressed in jeans and a T-shirt. Like Ernest, I didn't say anything. Nor did I run out after him as he went back to his car to dump his wig. I stayed put in the easy chair as the Canadian ambassador patiently answered questions from an audience of university students in the studio. While everything at the time was fine between Canada and the States, strange things were happening in Missoula.

I don't remember exactly what I was thinking when he closed the door and left the apartment, but I knew he'd be back.

About fifteen minutes later he reappeared. He didn't have the wig on, and he was carrying a grocery bag in one hand, his high heels in the other. His look was a mix of penitent and sly as he made his way across the green carpet as quickly and as unobtrusively as possible. Dressed as he was, I thought he might have been waiting for me to say hello and ask him where he'd been, or who or what had inspired his taste in clothes. But my mind was a blank as I watched him move past the TV and tiptoe up the stairs to the bedroom. He looked so thoroughly masculine, so ridiculously *unfeminine* in a dress, with his shaved, muscular calves propelling him up the stairs, that I wondered just who it was he was trying to fool.

A couple of minutes later, after he'd showered and changed, he came back down, this time wearing his khaki slacks and a Lacoste polo T-shirt. He asked me if I'd had breakfast, and I told him that I'd been waiting for him. It was a weekday and I knew that he was late for work, so I suggested that he call his colleagues to let them know he'd be late. He said that it didn't matter; he was taking the day off, and seriously doubted if he'd ever go back there again, and he never did.

We headed out to a restaurant where we both ordered pancakes. Sitting next to me, he confessed that putting on nylons, dresses, and makeup made him feel better; that it calmed him down. He said that this was the name of the game when you suffered from manic depression. I politely agreed with everything he was saying, even though at the time, I didn't know much about transvestites, or about the family history of ambiguity when it came to gender identity. I just put it down to eccentric behavior.

I wasn't aware of the fact that both my father and my grandfather had been dressed as little girls when they were young. Nor did I know that when Ernest first met Pauline and her sister Jinny at a party, it was Jinny he was more interested in—even though

Jinny was a lesbian, and not at all impressed with my grandfather. Likewise, I had no idea that Pauline had once suggested that she and Ernest get their hair cut and dyed the same color, and that Ernest went along with it.

Of course, back then, had I been aware of the erotic foreplay that went on between my grandfather and his fourth wife, Mary Welsh—when Ernest wanted to be one of her "girls"—a few bells might have started to ring. In an entry made in Mary's diary, dated December 20, 1953, while he and his wife were in East Africa, Ernest wrote:

> She has always wanted to be a boy, and thinks as a boy without losing any femininity. If you should become confused on this you should retire. She loves me to be her girls [sic], which I love to be; at night we do every sort of thing which pleases her and pleases me . . . Mary has never had one lesbian impulse but has always wanted to be a boy. Since I have never cared for any man and dislike any tactile contact with men except the normal Spanish *abrazo* . . . I loved feeling the embrace of Mary which came to me as something quite new and outside all tribal law. On the night of December 19th, we worked out these things and I have never been happier.[8]

Ernest wasn't gay, nor, as far as I know, did he ever cross-dress as an adult in public, but had I ever seen a copy of that page from Mary's diary, I certainly would have viewed my father in a different light. No longer would I have thought of him as the family exception to Ernest's macho image.

There must have been reasons for my dad's behavior. Like everyone else, he had a history, which was a collage of personal experiences and people who'd had a profound impact on his life. He was very much his father's son, even if I didn't understand just how similar they were. There was a direct connection that went to the heart of Ernest's ambiguity, but in Missoula, I didn't have the tools to interpret what I was seeing.

Greg was shifting quickly into another manic phase, and in the days after our conversation at the restaurant, he became increasingly impulsive and touchy. I had to be careful of what I said, because just about anything could get him angry. He was itching for a fight, and living with him was like walking a tightrope over a volcano. I didn't know how long I'd be able to hold out and I was wondering if I should call my girlfriend Ornella and tell her not to come. I'd called her about a week before saying she could come down, but now I wasn't sure. Although he was dressing up as a woman, he was showing an interest in just about anyone under thirty with two legs and a uterus. Having her around might spark the gunpowder of his emotions.

After some thought, however, I decided to let our plans stand. About a week before we were planning to drive across the border into Canada to pick up Ornella, my dad tried to cash one of his ex-wife Valerie's checks in a 7-Eleven, signing her name while dressed in a cream satin blouse, a woolen skirt, and a brown wig—the kind of clothes that he thought gave him the appearance of a forty-something housewife. This got him arrested, but he was lucky. The judge, a retired Air Force colonel, was lenient, and released him because he was a doctor, and according to him, Montana needed doctors. Nevertheless, Greg was warned that this was the last chance he would get. The next time he would be thrown in jail and would be left to sit there until he decided to get counseling. My father seemed to take the warning to heart, and behaved himself—for a while.

We drove up to Canada, but when we met Ornella at the Greyhound bus station in Lethbridge, I could tell that it was not going to be a pleasant trip back. Greg had decided, either genuinely or as a way of provoking me, to start courting my girlfriend by presenting her with a bouquet of red roses, and saying (after he'd kissed her hand) that she was as pretty as he'd imagined her to be. Ornella was flattered, but I wasn't amused. Unfortunately, the situation just got worse—or more comical, depending on your point of view—as we went along. Driving back to Missoula, we passed through Glacier National Park, and at one point near a mountain pass, my dad stopped by the side of the road. I don't know how high up we were, but there were wildflowers everywhere, and Greg took the time to gather up some for Ornella.

"I don't know what he's waiting for," Greg said as he handed her his selection, roots and all, "but if he doesn't propose to you soon, I will."

I was furious, but managed to control myself. He was provoking me where he was pretty sure he'd get a response. He was competing with me, as he often did with his sons, but this wasn't a game of tennis. My wig-wearing, cross-dressing dad was throwing down the gauntlet and asking if I was man enough to keep this attractive Canadian. I should have laughed in his face, but I was confused, and didn't know what to do at first. I loved and respected my father, and yet here he was trying to romance Ornella. It was not normal behavior, I told myself. He was nearing the peak of his manic phase, and luckily my instincts told me that I had to keep cool, no matter what. Eventually, after we'd left Glacier and were driving past Flathead Lake, he fell apart. He reached a point where his manic energy ran out of steam and he fell asleep. He stayed that way, slumped over in the backseat of the car, until we got to Missoula.

When I pulled into the parking lot he was awake, and in his apartment he suggested that we all go out to eat. By that time I'd had enough, and told him so. He left. Early the next morning when he reappeared, he asked if we felt like going to the cafeteria.

I refused, and this time he slammed the front door as he went out. I was relieved that he'd gone, and hoped that if he drove around for a while, maybe he'd cool down, get a grip, and we could all put what had happened behind us.

But I found out later that he'd been aggressive at the cafeteria, deliberately walking in without a shirt, behavior clearly prohibited by the sign on the front door. The lady at the cash register politely told him that he would have to leave, and my father, argumentative and enraged, kicked the glass door at the entrance, making it shatter. He spent the rest of the day driving around town, trying to find a place where he could cash a check for $5,000 that he'd received from his father's estate. It was a Saturday, and no one would do it for him. He came back around midnight when Ornella and I were asleep.

The next morning he was arrested. He came upstairs to the bedroom and told me a policeman was downstairs, and he had to go. He whispered to me because he didn't want to wake Ornella. "I'll be in touch," he said, and I watched him walk out to the police car in the parking lot.

As promised, the judge told him that he could stay in jail until he decided to go to a stress-management clinic in Butte. My father, who was dressed in the regulation orange jumpsuit that all the prisoners wore, refused to recognize the authority of the court, and sent scribbled messages to the judge saying that if he didn't let him out, he'd fire him. The judge smiled, but between puffs on his cigarette, told my father that he'd had enough of his nonsense and that his choice was clear.

Afterwards I talked to the judge outside the courtroom.

"John," he said, "your father is not gay." Of that he was sure, and he wanted me to know this fact. He'd read the police reports from Jordan and intended to get him the help he needed. Greg resisted this for two weeks before capitulating and agreeing to go to the clinic. By that time Ornella and I were camping outside town in a forest. We didn't have any money to pay the rent, and had been forced to leave the apartment when my dad was in jail. We had pitched a tent not too far from the river where we could wash and get water for cooking. It was very quiet, and at night we'd lie out in a clearing and look at the stars. When Greg was finally given a few days' leave from the clinic, he came back to Missoula and I drove him out to our campsite.

"This is living," he said, as he sat with me next to the river, calm, and finally off his manic high. "You guys don't know how lucky you are."

I knew then that he was thinking of his father and of the one untroubled time in his life.

SIMILARITIES

One of the most remarkable things about my grandfather is his continuing popularity. Many other American writers have won the Pulitzer or the Nobel Prize, but I don't think any of them approach the level of public acclaim Ernest still enjoys to this day. In an age when icons are dethroned with blinding speed, Ernest Hemingway's image endures. The simple and yet vivid quality of his writing has withstood the test of time, and the public's interest in his life and adventures is perhaps even stronger today than when he died.

As a boy, and later on as a teenager and young adult, I have to admit that I was often at odds with this powerful image. The heroic Hemingway myth didn't quite describe my family reality. Trying to find my own way in life, with a schizophrenic mother and a cross-dressing father, I was constantly reminded by my grandfather's fans that Ernest was still The Man. But how could I ever explain my father to these fans? Ernest Hemingway, like Teddy Roosevelt, John Wayne, and Clint Eastwood, was a standard, a measure of what it was to be an American male. And then there was my dad, walking into a cowboy bar in eastern Montana in drag. While this demonstrated a certain kind of bravery, it didn't make him another John Wayne.

Greg had more in common with his father's writing than with his personal myth. Ernest's stories were almost always tragic, with tough men like Robert Jordon and Harry Morgan achieving heroic status in their dignified response to overwhelming odds and inevitable defeat. It was a literature of loss, realistically portraying against his landscapes of love and war the hard truth that the world was essentially indifferent. It didn't care what happened to you, and the only thing that could redeem you was your personal code of ethics. We would all be broken by the world, impartially, but if we survived we would be, as Ernest wrote in *A Farewell to Arms*, "strong in the broken places." Written by a man who came from a country where being number one was, and continues to be, of paramount importance, this philosophy was almost subversive. This was something that had a lot more to do with my father than all the macho posturing Ernest was famous for. It was a statement that went against the grain of the nationwide belief that anyone with enough talent and hard work could overcome adversity and rise to the top of the heap. But myth is stronger than reality, and for most people—especially those who've never read any of his books—what comes to mind upon hearing the name Ernest Hemingway is not the social critic but the macho hero: the great hunter, the fisherman, the warrior, the lover. He was the man who did just about everything, and did it better than anyone else. This is what I usually heard growing up in Miami, and what I still hear today.

As a teenager living with my great-uncle Leicester and his family on Miami Beach, I tried to put together the pieces of a puzzle that just wouldn't fit. There was this enormous distance between my masculine grandfather and my father, with his passion for feminine fashion. I needed to understand just who I was in this family, and I'd started to ask questions: Who did I have more in common with—the cross-dressing dad or the famous grandfather—and how were these two men connected? What had gone wrong with Greg? Why was he a manic-depressive, and why did he have this strange need to dress up as a woman? My father had once said that "Papa was just too macho to be believed." But seeing that there didn't seem to be anyone else who shared this opinion, I had started to think that maybe what the rest of the family was saying was true—that Greg was just a black sheep.

For many in my family, and for all the people who had to deal with his unpredictable behavior, it was probably the easiest explanation. Greg was fundamentally flawed. He was a bad apple, perhaps even from birth, but one that took nothing away from the greatness of his father. Ernest couldn't be blamed, or even compared to his youngest son. Every family had a reject or two, and it was nothing to be ashamed of. Still, it was hard for me to accept this—in part because I thought it so insulting to a person I cared deeply about, and also, because I still believed there had to be a connection between the two.

And in fact there was. While most people continue to see Ernest Hemingway much as they've always seen him, critical opinion regarding his work and character has changed radically over the years. Starting in the late 1970s, but especially with the publication of *The Garden of Eden* in 1986, scholars began to focus on another side of Hemingway's personality and writing. It can no longer be denied that there is a lot more to Hemingway than meets the eye.

As a story, *The Garden of Eden* represented a departure from the usual Hemingway fare of rugged men in exotic locales. The French and Spanish locations were exotic enough, but the protagonist, young American writer David Bourne, had more on his mind than hunting, fishing, and war. David and his wife Catherine engage in a series of what might be defined as "transvestic" or gender-bending experiments. In the opening chapter, the two of them are very much in love, and after the publication of David's first successful novel, they spend some time in a small town on the southern coast of France. During the day they fish and swim and tan and make love, and David is very happy with this state of affairs. For him, it is the paradise alluded to in the book's title. But Catherine, much like the original Eve, isn't as satisfied with this idyllic existence, and changes everything when she pays a visit to David's barber:

> She came quickly to the table and sat down and lifted her chin and looked at him with laughing eyes and the golden face with the tiny freckles. Her hair was cropped as short as a boy's. It was cut with no compromises. It was brushed back, heavy as always, but the sides were cut short and the ears that grew close to her head were clear and the tawny line of her hair was cropped close to her head and smooth and sweeping back. She turned her head and lifted her breasts and said, "Kiss me please."[9]

David kisses her, and she tells him to check it out, to run his fingers through her hair and to see how it feels, which he does. And she tells him, "That's the surprise. I'm a girl. But I'm a boy too and I can do anything and anything and anything."[10] David at first doesn't quite know what to think, but accepts Catherine's new look and notices how the villagers react to his wife's appearance. They are very curious, and David realizes that her new haircut probably pushed things just a bit too far. Paris was one thing, the narrator says, but out in the countryside, it could be considered either very beautiful or just "too much."

In the evening, after a steak dinner with a great red wine, David and Catherine go back to their room and resume their lovemaking, but with a twist. Instead of the usual foreplay, she tells

David to forget about her breasts and to feel her cheeks and the back of her neck instead.

> *"Oh it feels so wonderful and good and clean and new. Please love me the way I am. Please understand and love me."*
>
> *He had shut his eyes and he could feel the long light weight of her on him and her breasts pressing against him and her lips on his. He lay there and felt something and then her hand holding him and searching lower and he helped with his hands and then lay back in the dark and did not think at all and only felt the weight and the strangeness inside and she said, "Now you can't tell who is who, can you?"*
>
> *"No."*
>
> *"You are changing," she said. "Oh you are. You are. Yes you are and you're my girl Catherine. Will you change and be my girl and let me take you?"*
>
> *"You're Catherine."*
>
> *"No, I'm Peter. You're my wonderful Catherine. You're my beautiful lovely Catherine. You were so good to change. Oh thank you, Catherine, so much. Please understand. Please know and understand. I'm going to make love to you forever."*[11]

As vague as it is, this scene gives you a pretty clear idea of what they're up to. I remember that my first reaction when I read it was more or less, "Well, then . . . Greg wasn't the only bad apple." Ernest wasn't cross-dressing like his son, but he was certainly thinking like him. It's true that in the novel Catherine pays a price for her increasingly obsessive sexual fantasies, and eventually goes insane. Eating the forbidden fruit does have its risks, and in the published Scribner version, Catherine is replaced by her lesbian lover, Marita, who then falls in love with David, bringing the story back into a heterosexual dimension. But that, I think, was my family and Ernest's editors trying to (posthumously) clean up Ernest's act, presenting him in a more traditional, "Hemingwayesque" fashion. The original manuscript wasn't as whitewashed, and Marita picks up where Catherine left off in the gender-bending games.

The publication of this book marked open-hunting season on the "androgynous" nature of the characters. Kenneth Lynn speculates that the androgyny in this novel (and in other Hemingway stories) is due to the fact that as a boy, my grandfather was "twinned" with his older sister, Marcelline. He wore the same female clothes she did, and in general was treated like a girl, going everywhere and doing everything his sister did for a longer-than-normal period of time. When I was at my great-uncle Leicester's house, I remember seeing some of these photographs of Ernest dressed up as a little girl, and thinking that it was strange. I asked Leicester's wife Doris why his parents made him go around like that. "It was something that people did back then," she told me. "It was no big deal."When I finally found out about my father's cross-dressing, I had already made the connection between the two, and decided that if Ernest had worn dresses as a boy, then logically, my father must have done the same, although as far as I know, he didn't. Years later, I believed that since my father had so much in common with Ernest, it followed that Ernest must have been a lot like his own father, Clarence. But that wasn't the case. Instead, Ernest's mother Grace was responsible for molding the man who would one day change the face of world literature and inspire millions of readers with his tales of *abnegazione,* or self-sacrifice. Grace had the drive and single-minded intensity that Ernest was famous for. Clarence may have taught his oldest son how to hunt and fish, but the boy's talent and ambition came from his mother.

As a young woman Grace had studied to become an opera singer; she even performed at the old Madison Square Garden in

New York City. Soon thereafter, she decided to give up her promising career and marry the man who had taken care of her mother while she was dying of cancer. She did not, however, become the happy housewife. For the most part, the servants (and occasionally Clarence, who liked to cook) prepared the meals and did the cleaning, while Grace attended to their children and to the music lessons she gave, which were netting her $1,000 a month compared to her husband's $50 as an obstetrician] She had a very clear idea of what her priorities were, and had more in common with her cosmopolitan father than she did with her husband.

Biographer Mark Spilka shows how the Victorian literature of that period reflected the desire of many women to play a greater role in society, something that Grace certainly aspired to. She was a proud, independent woman who probably resented the fact that as a child, she'd always played second fiddle to her brother Leicester. Raising her son as a twin to his older sister (with identical dolls and china tea sets), she subconsciously made up for this past injustice and created the early androgynous environment of Ernest's life.

Spilka sees the influence of women everywhere in Hemingway's work, and says the pervasive male-oriented image of my grandfather that he and many others had grown up with was in serious jeopardy.

> It is not simply the new feminism that asks us to judge more carefully Hemingway's dubious (i.e.; abusive, triangulated, exploitive) relations with women, and with the more feminine aspects of himself, or the androgynous aspects that, like so many men, he found so hard to cope with. It is his own central role in the creation and perpetuation of cultural myths and codes that are now under scrutiny from many angles, chief among which is the myth of men without women.[12]

In truth, there was never a time when Ernest could have real-istically thought of himself as being apart from women, or some kind of male in its pure essence. To the day he died, there was always a woman by his side.

Even when he did write exclusively about men, the relation-ships he depicted were often far from unambiguous. In "A Sim-ple Inquiry" (*Men Without Women*, 1927), a homosexual Italian major stationed on the Austrian front during World War I dis-creetly interrogates his enlisted orderly regarding his sexual preferences. The major asks the orderly, Pinin, if he has ever loved a woman, and the young orderly, being evasive, tells him that he has "been with girls." The soldier, in an isolated outpost in the Alps, is completely at the mercy of his commanding offi-cer. He cannot simply refuse to answer the major's questions. The major then asks him if he is in love now. Pinin tells him that he is, but that he doesn't write to his fiancée. The major at that point repeats the question, asking Pinin if he is absolutely sure of his love for the girl, and the orderly says that he is; the major isn't convinced, however, and wants to know if he is "corrupt." Pinin says that he doesn't know what the major means by "cor-rupt," and the major tells him that he "needn't act superior." "You're a good boy, Pinin," says the major. "But don't be supe-rior, and be careful that someone else doesn't come along and take you."

The orderly is dismissed, walking awkwardly or differently than before, and as Hemingway scholar Charles J. Nolan argues,

> These reactions come either because he has been under pressure
> or because he is embarrassed at being thought homosexual or be-
> cause he is upset at being propositioned or because he has been
> discovered . . . The story then ends in a way that drives us back
> into it. When the major hears Pinin return with more wood, he

thinks: "The little devil . . . I wonder if he lied to me." Once more
we ask ourselves questions about the major and his orderly.

Like other stories in Men Without Women, *this one calls*
upon our deepest understanding of human behavior. All three
of the characters are enigmatic revealing to us their complex
natures only after we have looked carefully at what they do and
say. Part of Hemingway's genius was to provide people [and]
arid situations for us that are as full of ambiguity as any we
find in our own experience. As the major observes, life is indeed
"complicated"—in the army and elsewhere.[13]

Nancy R. Comley and Robert Scholes further muddy the crystal waters of the myth of the Hemingway male in their exploration of the androgynous quality of Ernest's writing, describing it more specifically as "a metamorphic shift of race and gender."[14] To illustrate their point, they focus on a passage from the original manuscript of *The Garden of Eden*, later removed. In it the two protagonists are compared to *The Metamorphoses*, Rodin's famous statue of two lesbian lovers.

Referring to the statue, Catherine asks David if they look like
it now and David tells her that they do. She then insists, telling
him to "please be that way," and he says "how?" She tells him that
she wants him to change and to be her girl and to allow himself to
be taken. He wants her to be a bit more specific, and she repeats
what she told him before; that this can be done by changing, by
being her girl and by letting himself be taken. She then asks him
a second time if he will be like he was in the statue. At that point,
he finally understands and says that they are like the statue, of
which there were no photographs or reproductions. Clearly satis-
fied, she says that David is changing and that he has become her
girl, "Catherine."[15]

For Comley and Scholes, Ernest was clearly fascinated by Rodin's example of lesbian eroticism, but was equally excited by the idea of metamorphosis.[16] Perhaps fearing the criticism that their study of my grandfather's views on gender would provoke, they ask at the end of their book: "Have we been trying to show that Hemingway was gay?" No, they say. If anything, that was much too simple a question. Bisexuality, lesbianism, and sexual metamorphosis were all issues that Ernest and other artists of that period were aware of. As an intellectual you couldn't help but breathe in the cultural questions of the age, and other sexual practices were certainly part of the melting pot of ideas.[17]

Their description of my grandfather—that he was much too complex a person to describe as being simply gay or hetero—reminds me a lot of my own father. Like Ernest, Greg struggled for most of his life to deal with his own contradictions and to create a balance between the hypermasculine and the hidden female sides of his personality. The conflict must have been unbearable, but I don't think that his sex change helped resolve any of his problems. It was something he'd wanted for a long time, perhaps hoping that it would cure him of his mood swings, but when he could finally call himself "Gloria" and had the external anatomy to prove it, psychologically he was still the same old Greg. There was no rebirth, and he continued to be alternately plagued by periods of mania and depression. Like Ernest, he never did find the key to happiness. But just as my grandfather's work owes part of its complexity and modern appeal to its androgynous quality, representing as it does the attempt to portray men who are more in tune with their feminine sides, the same could be said for my father's own "metamorphosis." It didn't work for him, but as a symbolic act, perhaps he was just picking up where my grandfather had left off, taking Ernest's literary and nighttime fantasies to their logical conclusion.

Many biographers have written about my grandfather's fixation with hair. He wrote about it extensively: the cutting and dyeing of it; the way it felt against his hands; its color, the way it flowed, how it could be silky or not; if it was long or short, blond or red, boyish or like a girl's. It was a topic, strangely enough, that he was passionate about, along with bullfighting and deep-sea fishing. While it's not something that I get too excited about, Ernest did find it exciting—very much so. This literary fascination takes scholar Carl P. Eby into unexplored territory. In his book *Hemingway's Fetishism,* he admits that it's no longer "fashionable" to pick over a writer's subconscious while analyzing his work, but states that because of the "iceberg" principle inherent in Hemingway's writing, there is a lot that remains hidden in his words, and therefore, a psychoanalytic approach is justified.

Without a doubt, Eby leaves no stone unturned. In his psychoanalytic fervor he covers everything from "phallic women" to the relationship between "perversion, pornography, and creativity." He unearths a mountain of information on everything from Ernest's short stories to the last of his posthumous works. But again, what I found most useful were the similarities that I could see with my father. In particular when I got to the passage ". . . A failure of satisfactory maternal care, the mother either depriving or overwhelming the infant, makes a fertile ground for the later development of perverse tendencies . . ."[18] I thought *bingo*—the missing link.

Finally I was able to make a connection between the ways Greg and Ernest had been raised. It really had nothing to do with wearing girls' clothing, but instead with the fact that Grace and Pauline had both prevented their sons from fully recognizing their own masculinity in those crucial first three years of development. Another piece of the puzzle had fallen into place. Ernest was certainly "overwhelmed" by his mother, and Pauline lacked what my dad called the "maternal instinct." When Greg was born, Pauline's relationship with Ernest had lost its initial passion. She had failed in her attempt to give him the daughter he'd wanted, and had handed over her second son's upbringing to their governess, Ada. Knowingly or not, she had deprived Greg of the love that he craved, effectively damaging him.

To deal with the anger and confusion that he felt for his mother and with the stress of his later manic periods, Greg in his cross-dressing seems to have taken his cue from Ernest. Eby suggests that his father's fetish for hair was used to negotiate moments of crisis and extreme stress. In the spring of 1947 Ernest was about as stressed as he could get. His wife Mary was in Chicago taking care of her father, whose doctors were recommending castration as a cure for prostate cancer. Ernest's son Patrick had been in bed for a month at the Finca Vigía, Ernest's home in Cuba, ranting like a madman after a car accident left him with a head-trauma psychosis. Ernest, taking care of Patrick almost around the clock, was suffering from the combined effects of lack of sleep, worry about his son, loneliness from being without Mary, and the usual heavy drinking. Something had to be done to ward off another "black-ass period," as he called his depressive bouts, and he decided to dye his hair red. Not that it was the first time. In 1933 he had written to my grandmother Pauline, asking her how to change his hair from red to blond.[19] Red hair, according to his older sister Marcelline, had a special significance to Ernest, in that Grace had always referred to "reddish" hair as the nicest color on a woman.[20] Both Kenneth Lynn and Carlos Baker wrote that my grandfather's excuse for the bright copper-red of his hair was that he had mistakenly used a bottle of Martha Gellhorn's shampoo, left over from when she had lived there. In a letter to Mary, however, we get a completely different version:

Last night I . . . had to make the all night standby [Patrick's bed] and thought you would be coming back soon and what [I] could do to amuse me and please you and remembered how you used to talk about Catherine in the night and how her hair was and so decided would make red—So started on a test piece with just the drab—and only tiny bit of mixture and it made fine red in about 35 minutes—(I was checking on Mousie [Patrick] all the time.) Hair as dark as mine has to go through red before can be blond—So I thought, what the hell. I'll make it really red for my kitten and did it carefully and good, same as yours, and left on 45 minutes and it came out as red as a French polished copper pot or a newly minted penny—not brassy—true bright coppery—and naturally in the morning I was spooked shitless—and then thought what the hell—with everything the way it is and we free people able to do anything we want that doesn't hurt other people, whose business is it but yours and mine—

So I just had red hair—and I loved it for you and was proud of it—and nobody said anything about it more than they said to Gen. Custer when he wore his down to his shoulders. Because right now have quite a little credit with my troops . . .

So now I am just as red-headed as you would like your girl Catherine to be and don't give a damn about it at all— (like very much). It's not deep red—but light, bright, coppery, like shiny copper pans—and I'll do it again before you come home—or do it again when you get here . . . If a girl has a right to make her hair red I have—I've fought enough fights so no one can say anything to me . . . except maybe really wonderful fighting people and maybe they didn't fight as many times over such a long space of years and months and days—

So I will be red-headed kitten when I see you and very proud to be and hope will please my kitten—

Actually me and Catherine both would be better dark red than this jolly new copper tinker's colour. But you can't do that at home.[21]

When I first read the part where Ernest says that naturally in the morning, he was "scared shitless," I had to laugh. It reminded me so much of my father. Not that my father was into dyeing his hair (he usually wore wigs), but the words that Ernest uses are so reminiscent of Greg. I had often seen my dad pass from macho to a state of panic and back again. Panicking at the mess he'd made of things in a manic phase, worrying what others would think, and then, just like his father, saying "what the hell" and being proud of the way he was dressed or of what he'd done. For me, reading a letter like the one above is a kind of homecoming. It takes me back to the man my father was, reminding me of his craziness, but also of his fragility and his humor. He was very much the mirror image of his father. Two men trying to incorporate the other half, obsessed by women, creating a special bond with each other that my father knew no one would understand, and that would remain a secret to the day he died. After all, who would have believed him had he shouted out, "Papa was a gender-bending, earring-wearing, hennaed kind of guy!" No one, of course. Ernest's image as a pillar of American manhood was—and remains—untouchable. I only wish that these scholars had been more successful in publicizing their updated portrait of my grandfather while my father was still alive. Myth, it's true, is a hard thing to battle, but I'm sure that it would have helped Greg to know that the general public was finally aware of what he'd been hinting at for years.

Chapter 7

LES AND DORIS

My father's uncle Leicester and his wife Doris had a house on the southern tip of San Marino Island, between Miami and Miami Beach. They'd bought it with the last of the advance Les had received for the biography of his brother Ernest, and they stayed there from the early 1960s to the mid-1980s. It was the oldest house on the island, Spanish colonial in design, with a front yard that looked out to the bay. In 1974 it had a very lived-in look, with flaking paint and a driveway that badly needed repaving. Les and his family weren't big on gardening, and aside from occasionally mowing the lawn or trimming the Australian pines, you really felt as if you'd discovered a secret jungle when you pulled up to the place. There was a riot of vegetation that contrasted starkly with the manicured lawns and hedges of the other houses on the island. Here nature was given a free rein, and while Les probably could have done something to bring his budding rain forest to heel, only once did he ever try.

In general, he had more important things to do. A very outgoing person, Les was full of optimism and ideas that were going to make us all rich someday. He was certainly one of the luckiest men I've ever met, even if his plans never did strike it big. He wasn't very good at business. Fundamentally he was a generous man, giving away more than he ever received, so I'm not surprised that when he got the call from the young priest who was trying to find us a place to stay, he and Doris immediately offered to take us in. We were family, Les said, and that was all he needed to know. "I will not allow three of my brother's grandchildren to end up in an orphanage," was how he'd settled the matter.

I was happy that all of us would stay together, and that we wouldn't be parceled off to different foster homes, which was one of the options the priest had given me. I even got to bring my dog, Scotty, a six month old Sheltie that my mother had bought me before she decided to take a vacation from her maternal duties. The priest had had a mental list of potentially receptive relatives, but when he'd asked me about my father I didn't think that we would be going there. Greg and Valerie's apartment on East 87th Street in Manhattan was already cramped with their three children, Sean, Edward and Vanessa, and Brendan (whose father was the Irish playwright Brendan Behan). Valerie had made arrangements to get us sent somewhere else in 1971, so going back there two years later just wasn't in the offing. At this point, Greg already wanted to move out West, where he would have been able to afford a bigger house and thus take care of all of his children (or at least, that was the dream). But his wife was in love with the Big Apple, and she knew how to keep her husband's impulses at bay. As it turned out, living with Uncle Les and his family on Miami Beach was a much better alternative for us.

For starters, the house was enormous, bigger than anything my parents had ever rented. I shared a room with my brother Pat on the second floor. Our beds and all the furniture were antiques from the 1930s and '40s. The lady who sold the house to Les and Doris had wanted to get rid of everything, so in addition to the grand piano in the sunken living room, they were also given the library with its complete collection of encyclopedias and yearbooks, running up to 1944. I had moved into a time capsule, a testament of how the better half had lived, but one that was slowly falling apart in the subtropical heat. The iron fittings of the windows facing the bay were being held together in many places by the putty on the panes. The sea air rusted everything, and we were told not to open those windows for fear that forever after you'd never be able to close them. The external walls of the house were incredibly thick, and even though a good part of the plaster needed replacing, in the summer the insulation they provided made it cooler than many of the newer houses on the island.

We usually ate in the dining room, right next to the living room and facing the bay, with Les sitting at the head of the table, Doris at the other end, and the rest of us in the middle. Sometimes Les would barbecue steaks out on the porch, and sometimes we'd spear the lobsters that hid in the holes of the seawall, serving them up after they'd been popped in a pot of boiling water.

My Uncle Les was a big man, six feet tall, who bore a great physical resemblance to his brother Ernest. I was always amazed (skinny thirteen-year-old that I was) at the quantity of food that he could put away. When he made chicken paella with Cuban yellow rice (Les did a lot of the cooking), he would literally pile up his plate with a steaming mountain of rice. He might share an occasional glass of wine with his wife, but he wasn't much of a drinker, and I can't ever remember him being drunk.

Of course the greatest thing about the house was being on the water. Doris used to say that she would never give up the place because sitting out on the lawn and watching the sun go down after work was something that she couldn't do without. The sky would turn bright shades of orange and red, and when it got dark you could see the lights from the houses across the bay.

Hilary, the younger daughter of Les and Doris, had built a makeshift dock with a few planks out to the pilings. Les usually had a boat out there, either one of his own or a friend's, or just one that he was fixing up to sell. In 1974 when I went to live with them, I remember that for a few weeks, an enormous sixty-foot ex-PT boat from World War II was tied up at the dock. The owner was a young hippie from Michigan called Farley. He had bought the boat, which had been converted into a cabin cruiser, somewhere along the Miami River. He was fixing it up, hoping to live in it with his girlfriend and little boy while cruising the Caribbean. Farley was painting it black, and the color gave it a very heavy-metal feel. The boat was made out of wood, and Uncle Les had his doubts about its seaworthiness. It was too top-heavy, he said, and he was right.

When Farley finished the paint job and left with his girlfriend and heir for the Bahamas, we saw him by chance that morning as he was steaming up the government cut toward the Gulf Stream. The bow and the stern were bobbing wildly up and down in the light chop, and Les joked that if Farley wanted to kill himself, he had a right to do so, but that taking innocent women and children along with him was a crime.

At the other end of the spectrum in terms of the quality of the boats that were docked in front of Les's house was the 1930s Great Lakes schooner that belonged to a businessman from Georgia. It was about fifty feet long and had beautiful lines, with teak decks and a bowsprit that reminded me of clipper ships and ports that I could only read about. The owner was restoring it to use as his personal yacht, but when he finally took it out for a test run he discovered that it had a problem when it came to navigating the Miami area. The keel on this boat was very deep, which is good for the Great Lakes but bad for Miami because of the shallow water. He ran aground at least five times on the afternoon he tried to take it over to Coconut Grove. He eventually sold the boat, realizing that he'd never be able to use it the way he wanted to. It remains to this day one of the most beautiful vessels I've ever laid eyes on, and convinced me, if I ever needed convincing, that I had to have a sailboat.

Problem was that neither Les nor Doris had the money to buy me one. I was thinking of a Sunfish, and they suggested I write to my dad for the cash. So I got some paper, a pen, and a clipboard, and sat out on the seawall to write a letter. I didn't know it then, but if you wanted to impress or in some way have an impact on my father, the best way to do it was to write him a letter. Anyone could make a phone call, but to sit down and write out something that made sense—and, what's more, sounded good when you read it—now that was difficult, and he appreciated the effort that went into it. He might not agree with what you were saying or asking for, but nine times out of ten, a well-written letter would put him in a generous mood if he had any money. My father was an MD, but he was also the son of a writer, and reading and the written word were inevitably things that reminded him of Ernest.

My letter was about a page long, front and back, and apart from asking him how he was and assuring him that I was doing well in school, the rest of it had to do with my plans for the boat, and why I loved the sea. I spent an afternoon trying to express what anyone who's grown up near the ocean and has sailed understands—that the sea becomes a part of you, and for the rest of your life, even if you move to where the waves can't be heard, the sea is never too far away. All it takes is one day out on a boat with a good wind and the years spent in exile disappear. Everything comes back to you: the way it once felt, the salt spray, the beauty, and the closest thing to freedom I've ever experienced, racing over the liquid edge between water and air.

Looking back on it, I can see now how important that letter was. Les and Doris were never anything but kind and generous to me, but at thirteen, I was always acutely aware who my real parents were, and why I wasn't living with them. My father had his other family in New York, and my mother had dropped off the radar screen. She was traveling again, alone with her voices, just one step ahead of the people who, in her mind, never seemed to tire of stalking her. Without a doubt, being a teenager and having to deal with all the normal problems of adolescence was hard enough, but when you combined these with my mother's unpredictability and the helplessness that I felt with her schizophrenia, it's no wonder that I loved sailing. At least out on the water I could control the boat's direction.

I sent the letter off, and my father wrote back about a week later. I think he found my heroic sea imagery a bit overdone, but it was a nice reply, and he'd included a check for the Sunfish. I then looked through the classifieds of *The Miami Herald* and found a man who was selling one for $90. It was five years old and painted a dark blue. The modern versions of this boat are very light, but this thing weighed a ton in comparison. It was a pre–oil embargo model, and the fiberglass was a lot thicker. Les managed to bargain the price down another $10, and then with some rope and old blankets, we tied it onto the roof of the car and hauled it back to the house.

I think that for the first couple of months I must have sailed every day after school. I took it everywhere in the bay, and eventually went as far out as the Rickenbacker Causeway. In the summer I'd set off in the early morning, sometimes not returning till sunset, and never wearing anything more than a pair of khaki-colored gym shorts. I was deeply tanned, and I remember my cousin Anne saying that I looked "black."

Occasionally I took my brother and sister out, but mostly I was on my own. My brother Pat was going to the elementary school across the street from my junior high school. He was in second grade and a little wild man, very energetic and bordering on hyperactive, but very smart. My sister had learning problems, had always had them, and while my mother had initially paid for special teachers, later on with all the paranoiac moving and school changes, Maria's learning disabilities were effectively neglected. In Miami Beach she was put into the fifth grade, instead of the sixth grade class where she should have been placed.

At the end of the school year my mother showed up at the house and said that she wanted us back. I wasn't in a mood to leave, so only Maria and Patrick went with her. She had rented an apartment in North Miami Beach, and I thought that would be the end of it. But about a month later she phoned and asked if the kids could stay at Les and Doris's house for a week. She didn't give a reason why (my mother could be fairly enigmatic when she wanted to be), although she was probably having another crisis. I can't remember what Les and Doris thought of her request, but in the end Les drove over to their apartment to pick up my brother and sister. In the month that the kids had been with her, she'd gone from bad to worse, and was no longer worrying about groceries or keeping the house clean. Patrick and Maria said that they'd been forced to steal money from her purse to buy food, and that often they didn't know where she was. It was obvious to anyone looking at the situation that something had to be done. My mother needed help, and was certainly incapable of taking care of my brother and sister.

Over the years, many people I've spoken to from outside the family have found it hard to believe that the grandchildren of Ernest Hemingway could have faced these hardships. Even if our parents were having their fair share of mental problems, weren't there other relatives apart from Les and Doris who could have taken care of us? My father's brothers, for instance, or my mother's mother—all of whom, by any stretch of the imagination, were well off. Even in the days before Hemingway Ltd. and my family's wildly successful venture in marketing the name and image of Ernest with furniture, wallpaper, and salad dressing (to name but a few of the licensing categories), my father and uncles had a steady flow of money from the book rights. By law our situation should have been exclusively my father's problem, as he had legal custody over us, and while he may have wanted to do something—buy a big house for all his kids, or something along those lines—he didn't. Whether this was because his wife told him that another solution would have to be found, or because, like everyone else, he just didn't see our predicament as being that compelling, I'll never know. Whatever the case, I find it ironic that the man who was the least prepared economically and who was often ridiculed by the rest of the family as being a loafer and a dreamer was the one who did the most for us, and who really taught me what being generous was all about. Which just goes to prove that you *can* judge a person by his actions.

After talking with Doris, Leicester's younger son Peter agreed to keep Patrick. Peter was a psychology professor in Saskatchewan, Canada. He and his wife had two young boys of their own, and Doris thought it would be a wonderful opportunity for Patrick. While logically I had to agree, I can't say that I was happy about it. Since my parents' divorce, I'd moved around a lot, but even when I was going to boarding school or living with my father, I'd always known that my mother was there and that Patrick and Maria were with her, and that if I wanted to, I could always go back to them. But when Patrick was sent away, I suddenly realized that that would never again be the case. Bit by bit the old family was falling apart, and while I knew that my mother wasn't well and that my brother didn't have much of a choice, it didn't make the situation any easier.

About a year later it was Maria's turn. Not to Canada this time, but to Iowa. Doris had grown up there, and through her relatives, she'd contacted some friends of the family, a fifty-year-old farmer and his wife. They were good people and agreed to take Maria in. My sister lived with them for six months, but this new move, combined with her learning disabilities and all the other emotional problems that she had, caused her to be deeply resentful of her new family, and soon thereafter another home had to be found. This time she was sent to live with our father, who wasn't in New York but trying his luck as a doctor in Montana, on his own. Valerie still wouldn't budge from the Big Apple.

I don't think that Maria stayed with Greg for very long. It was during my father's first stab at life in the Big Sky State, and when that ended with the onset of another depression, he sent Maria to my mother in Los Angeles. Alice had gone out there to be closer to her father. She'd rented a small two-bedroom bungalow in the Wilshire district. I wouldn't see either of them for about three years.

To snap out of his depression, which seemed to have gotten worse upon his return to New York, my father came to Miami for a series of electroshock treatments. He was no stranger to electroshock therapy, having undergone it numerous times in the past. He even went so far as to recommend it to others when they were feeling down. My mother had had them, at his insistence, telling me later, "It was no big deal." My father liked to talk about the time when, as he described it, the technicians had fudged the anesthesia, administering the shocks when Greg was fully conscious of what was happening. The way he remembered it, you wouldn't think it was an experience he'd want to repeat, but he believed in the therapy and said that at times, it was the only thing that worked.

During the first two years that I lived with Les and Doris, I had my father placed firmly on a pedestal. He could do no wrong in my eyes, and even if he often did nothing—hoping that a problem would disappear on its own, or that someone else would deal with it—I didn't hold it against him. I blamed his inaction on Valerie or my mother, or on just about anything else. The important thing was that he existed, as an anchor, an idol. Everything else might go to hell, but he was strong; he still loved me, and I knew that I could count on him. The Sunfish that I had was proof of this. He listened to me, and if it wasn't an ideal situation, it was better than nothing.

Had I delved deeper into the family background, his resilience would have impressed me even more. In the 1970s, in addition to Ernest, his grandfather and his aunt Ursula had already killed themselves. Clarence's final battle with depression was brought on, apart from his financial problems, by a diabetes-induced gangrenous leg. In 1982, Leicester, who also suffered from diabetes, committed suicide after a long battle with this illness. His doctors had told him that both his legs would have to be amputated. Not wanting to become a burden to his family, he shot himself with a revolver at the front door of his house.

When he died, I remember that it was my grandmother who called me first. She was crying and told me that something terrible had happened; Leicester had killed himself, and she wanted me to know about it from a member of the family before I saw it on the evening news. Afterwards I phoned my father, and I remember how quiet his voice got when I told him. He'd had his disagreements with his uncle, but no matter how he might have felt about the man in the last years of his life, the news of his suicide must have hit him hard. He just kept repeating how sorry he was.

Fourteen years later my cousin Margaux died of a drug overdose. I was at home in Milan working on a translation and heard it on the radio. My first reaction was that it couldn't be true, that it was someone's idea of a very bad joke. It was July 1, 1996, the day before the anniversary of my grandfather's suicide, and I looked on the Internet to see if anyone was writing about it. Although an Associated Press article confirmed what I'd heard, I still kept thinking that it was surreal. She was more or less my age, and usually when people killed themselves in my family, they were in their sixties. Margaux was not someone I expected to die so early, and it really shook me up. All I could remember was the way I'd seen her when she was a teenager, so rowdy and full of life. The idea of her killing herself just didn't fit.

The press, of course, had a field day with her suicide. They'd always liked to talk about the "Hemingway curse," as if my great-grandfather Clarence had made some sort of Faustian pact with the devil, and now that they had Margaux to throw into the pot, it was even better. She was the golden girl, the million-dollar model and the *Babe* perfume spokesperson. I had my own ideas about the so-called curse, and believed it had more to do with genetics and bad luck than with voodoo. Either you had the genetic tendency for being bipolar, or you didn't. Some got lucky, while others weren't. Margaux suffered from it; I didn't.

My first real taste of the mental demons on the Hemingway side of the family, and not just on my mother's side, came in 1975. I hadn't seen my father since Christmas of 1973, when he took Maria, Patrick, and me down to Bimini for a long weekend. On that trip, I remember that it rained all the time, and that he had read me a page from the memoir he was writing, asking me what I thought. It was bitter prose, with lines about "Papa kicking fairies in the balls" and other such pleasantries. I said that it sounded great, although I really didn't have any idea what he was talking about. It was, as I was later to discover, but the tip of the iceberg of a rage that was always with him but that you rarely saw if he wasn't in a manic phase, or drunk. He kept it hidden as much as he could because he knew that no one would understand how he felt. Ernest was a literary legend, a giant among twentieth-century authors and admired the world over for what he'd written, and because of the mythic image that had grown up around him. You just couldn't speak badly of the man, especially if you were his son.

Like anyone else, there was nothing my father could do about the problems he'd inherited, but I can't help but think that his desperation and rage were like kerosene on the hot coals of his illness. They nourished his madness, and after a flare-up he'd come back to the reality that the rest of us lived, down from his manic high, pale and more confused. And that's how I remember him on the day that he was discharged from the clinic in 1975.

I was excited. I hadn't seen him for such a long time, and we were finally going to be together. Doris tried to prepare me, saying that he'd been in the hospital and that he wasn't in the best of shape, but I didn't care; he was coming to see me, and that was all that mattered. It was a typical sunny day in Miami, and Doris met him at the front door when he pulled up in a taxi. I was out by the water and ran to the house when I heard her call my name. My father had a small sports bag that he left in the hall, and was wearing a long-sleeved checkered shirt and khaki trousers. I thought the shirt was strange because it was hot, and he hadn't rolled up the sleeves. His hair was the same jet-black that I remembered, but disheveled. His face was tired and his lips dry and chapped.

"It's great to see you!" he said, hugging me in front of my aunt. Feeling him close, I thought that Doris was wrong. Whatever had happened to him, it couldn't have been that bad. He asked me how things were going, and I told him, "Not bad." I talked for a bit about my school and my friends, and he seemed content just to listen. We walked through the house and then over to the seawall where I'd left the Sunfish. I said that I used it almost every day and thanked him for the check.

"What check?" he asked.

"The one you gave me for the boat," I told him.

"I bought you the boat?"

"You don't remember? I wrote you a letter and you wrote back, sending a check with it."

"I gave you that?" And as listless as he was, not being able to remember this angered him.

"Absolutely," I said. "It's a great boat." I wondered why he couldn't remember, because I had the letter in my room and I'd seen the check.

"Well, then, I guess I did." And he explained that after a round of electroshock treatments, his memory was never that good. I didn't know exactly what the treatments did, nor the fact that they were used to cure depression, but he told me that it was no big deal and that he was probably in the *Guinness Book of World Records* by now for the number of times they'd strapped him down.

"But doesn't it hurt?" I asked.

"No. You really don't feel a thing, if they do it right," he said. Looking at his lips and his bloodshot eyes, I thought that maybe it did hurt, and that his doctors weren't very good. The idea of running a current through someone's brain seemed bizarre. Wasn't that how they executed people? In the state of Florida, that was how they did it. I was only fifteen, but the way he described it, with all the straps and sedatives, it seemed more like medieval torture than something doctors should be doing to their patients.

Afterwards my cousin Hilary came out with her Polaroid and asked if we wanted a picture.

"Sure," I said. My father put his arm around me and we both smiled as she said "Cheese." She handed us the photo and left as we waited for it to develop. I was happy to have a souvenir of our meeting. My father had a flight that afternoon to New York, and for all I knew, another two years might pass before I'd see him again.

When it was ready my father had a look at it, and then took a pen out of his pocket, scribbled something on the back, and gave it to me.

He'd written "Fuck us!"

"There," he said, "it's official." I don't think I said anything. I just looked at the two words and put the Polaroid in my pocket when he got up and told me that he had to leave. The anger and the bitterness of his message were obvious. He wasn't saying "Help me!" because they'd fried his brains and he couldn't remember where he was or what he'd done to deserve such a fate. No; he was saying "Fuck us," and that included me. I guess he had to give the Polaroid a context, a little something to help me remember him the way he'd been.

I walked with him through the house to the front hall and then waited in the driveway until the cab came. He hugged me again when he said good-bye, and I watched him go, my souvenir in hand.

Chapter 8

FORT BENTON

In the summer of 1977, Leicester's son Peter came down from Saskatchewan with his family and my brother Patrick. I hadn't seen Pat for three years, and was surprised at how much he'd changed. He was a lot taller, with longer hair, and he wore a pair of eyeglasses that gave him a more pensive look—or at least pensive for an eleven-year-old. They were there for a little over a month, and once again, Pat was up on the second floor in the bed next to mine. We were almost always together, and I noticed that he had changed in other ways. He was no longer the innocent little wild man he'd been at seven. The separation from our mom had worked it so that we had more in common, even if we would have been hard-pressed to explain just what that similarity was. In effect, we'd both been adopted, and even though the people who had taken us in were relatives and as generous as you could hope for, it wasn't the same as living with your own folks. Doris and Les had always done their best to make me feel a member of the family, but I knew how quickly things could change. I'd seen it happen with my mother. It was important, of course, to feel that you belonged, but deep down I knew that I couldn't count on it.

While Peter was there he helped his father out with odd jobs around the house that needed doing, and with a fishing boat that Les had picked up for cheap on the Miami River. The wooden Egg Harbor boat with twin gasoline engines was thirty years old, and, as was usually the case with my great-uncle's boats, in need of a lot of work. Les arranged to have it hauled out of the water in a boatyard in Coconut Grove, where the whole family spent the better part of a week in shifts, cleaning the planking of its community of barnacles and checking for dry rot, and then caulking and covering everything in a red, lead-based anti-fouling paint.

But that wasn't the end of it. Back at the house Peter discovered dry rot in one of the bulwarks at the bilge level, and decided that it needed replacing. He had a lot of experience in working with wood and Les was lucky to have him there. They figured that it wouldn't take them more than a day or two to cut a new one, but the dry rot that they discovered was just the beginning. There was a whole section that needed to be gutted and replaced, and in the cramped and humid working conditions, Peter ended up doing the lion's share of the job. His father had spent two weeks in intensive care the year before after a bad heart attack, and Peter didn't want to see him have another one in the August heat.

Outwardly Les was the picture of Hemingway health and vigor, but he was getting older, and that may have been one of the reasons that I had to leave after four years. I was two years away from university, and Doris and Les were thinking about my future and who would pay for my education. The obvious choice was my father. He had a lot more money than they did, and he was still my legal guardian.

Another contributing factor that might have led to my departure from Les's home was the bad blood that had flowed between him and my father. The problems stemmed from a legal spat that developed when my father promised Les a percentage of the royalties from his memoir in exchange for having ghostwritten a part of it. But when Greg reneged on their verbal agreement, Les threatened to sue him. I remember that Les put a lot of work into Greg's book, and while none of his writing was used in the end, my father had given his word, and Les didn't feel like forgetting that. Apparently, during a manic phase, Greg had done the same thing with many other people. I think what really galled Les was the fact that while my dad was complaining bitterly that "relatives don't sue each other," I was living with Les and being treated as a member of his family. My father may have promised away half (or all) of his royalties to various collaborators, but my great uncle shouldn't have been lumped together with everyone else. He was different, and by rights should have been treated differently, meriting a minimum of respect.

Only once did I ever hear Les talk about my dad's broken promise, and it was enough to understand that he was furious and felt cheated, yet at the same time embarrassed for having shown his anger. Doris and I were riding home with him from Miami, and just after we'd passed the tollbooth on the Venetian Causeway, I heard them talking about my father and the court case. I was sitting in the rear seat and casually mentioned that perhaps Greg wasn't entirely at fault. I was convinced that he wouldn't have tried to deceive his uncle on purpose, but I would have done better to keep my mouth shut. I had no idea how worked up Les had become about the case, and my comment was the straw that broke the camel's back.

"Greg knew damn well what he was doing!" Les shouted, and it was the first time that he'd ever raised his voice with me. He said that my dad hadn't kept his word and that there was absolutely nothing to be said in his defense. From that point onward, I didn't try. I kept my thoughts to myself.

Without a doubt my father had a talent for pricking people where it hurt them most, and while I'll probably never know if it was the mud-slinging over the agreement that wore out my welcome, Peter's return to Canada gave Les and Doris the soft departure they were looking for, with no sudden break or wrenching ultimatums. They knew that I wouldn't be happy when my brother finally left, so they asked me if I wanted to go with him— at least up to New York City where I could then spend the summer with my father.

We made the trip up the coast in two days, stopping the first night at a campground in Georgia. I remember that our tent was in a stand of pine trees, and that the humidity and heat were worse than what you got in Miami. It was the Deep South with a vengeance, without the slaves or the plantation owners, but with a white wooden gate and chain-link fence that locked us in at midnight.

The next morning at seven we were on the road again. We drove all day, and in the late afternoon we pulled up in front of Jake Hemingway's house in Maryland, just outside of the capital. Peter's older brother worked for the navy as an engineer, and had the tall, heavyset build shared by both Les and Ernest. He smoked a pipe, sported a crew cut, and played chess at killer levels. He reminded me of the 1950s, and the fact that he worked for the military, even as a civilian, seemed more than logical. He and his wife had two children, both in their teens, and I remember that one afternoon she took all of us into the capital to see the sights, including the Smithsonian, the Lincoln Memorial, and the National Air and Space Museum.

That same day we had dinner with Leicester's first wife (and Jake and Peter's mom), Patricia. She was a very intelligent, attractive woman who worked as a cartographer for the government. One of her hobbies was genealogy, and she'd done extensive research on the family, tracing it back to the first immigrants who'd arrived in the New World, and even earlier to the Hemingways of Leeds and Yorkshire in England. What I liked about her was her sense of humor and the way she listened, making you feel that everything you had to say was important.

Two days later, instead of driving me to my dad's apartment, Peter drove Pat and me over to Dulles Airport, where I took the shuttle to LaGuardia. At the airport Peter took us to the Eastern terminal and stayed with the van, while Pat and I went to the departure lounge and waited for about fifteen minutes before my flight was ready to board. I could tell that Pat was upset and on the verge of tears, but what could I do? My brother was only a boy, and certainly none of what passed for normal in our family was fair or as it should have been. We were always getting moved around. I hugged him tight when it was time to leave, and then walked down the ramp, trying not to look back as he waved goodbye in his T-shirt and shorts.

Once in New York I took a cab to the apartment on East 95th Street. I was sad about Pat, but on the bridge over the East River and in the uptown traffic, I tried to think of the things that I'd be able do that summer. Find a job or hang out in the museums or the park. Make some friends and perhaps find a girlfriend. I had to think positively that things would work out. It was a big town with a lot to offer, and of course, there was my dad and all the plans that he usually had.

I was familiar with the building where they lived because Doris had taken Hilary and me up there for Easter vacation earlier that year. We'd bought tickets on a Greyhound and stayed with Valerie and two of her kids. At the time I didn't know why she wanted us to go the city, other than to visit Val or to show Hilary where she'd worked as a young woman for *Newsweek*. Perhaps, though, it was just to get me used to the idea of going back, of eventually living with my father.

When the taxi pulled up in front of the building and the doorman helped me with my bag, I fully expected to see Greg waiting for me in one of his checkered shirts. I had been told that he would be there, but he wasn't. His wife was there instead, and while Valerie was friendly enough, I could tell that having me for the summer was not something that she had suggested.

I left my bag in the hallway of their tiny apartment and we sat down in the living room. She asked if I'd had a good trip up, and when I wondered aloud where everyone was, she said that she was the only one around. Greg was in Montana and the kids were either off in the countryside with friends, or at summer camp. There wouldn't, in fact, be much to do that summer, and I'd be pretty much left to my own devices. She didn't say as much, but she definitely gave me the impression that my being there didn't make much sense.

"Well, then, I guess I'll go back to Miami," I told her, and almost instantly I was standing in front of a happier woman. She repeated that I didn't have to go, but I said that I might as well, all things considered, and that was that. She booked another flight and in the evening I rode back out to the airport.

As fate would have it, I was just in time to take part in a chapter of the city's energy history. It was July 25, 1977, and as my plane was lined up on the runway behind about five others, suddenly all the lights went out. At first we waited, and then came instructions to take everyone back to the terminal, where we sat in our seats and were served drinks until the airport decided that the blackout was not temporary, and that everyone should go home. In the terminal everything was dark, and airport employees were wandering around with flashlights when they could find them. I gave Valerie a call and she suggested I take a cab back to the apartment, but I told her that I'd be fine where I was. I spent the night on the floor with hundreds of other stranded passengers.

I heard that there was looting in the city, but also a lot of partying, and instances of people doing their best to help each other out. In the airport all we could do was wait. Everyone who had spent the night there wanted to find a way home, but there were also incoming flights in the late morning, and Ernest's widow, Mary, was on one of them. I had finally been confirmed on another evening flight and I was walking in the direction of the gates (back then, there were no metal detectors or other security measures) when I saw what looked like a crowd of journalists moving around a small lady with white hair and tanned, wizened skin. I hadn't seen her since 1971, but she looked the same. Mary was quite well known after the publication of her book the year before, and she looked very VIP as she and her crowd glided past me. She had been my grandfather's caretaker, and the one who'd found him with his shotgun-splattered brains the morning that he'd killed himself. A tough lady, to be sure. While I couldn't say that I really knew Mary, both my mother and Valerie liked her. This was the last time I would ever see her.

In Miami I was picked up by Leicester's son-in-law, Bill. Dressed in shorts and a brightly colored Hawaiian shirt, he let me in on the fact that I wasn't supposed to be there. Les and Doris were not at all amused. New York was where I was supposed to have stayed. While they didn't say anything when we got back to the house (it was late and not a good time to talk), a few days later Doris did finally explain to me why I'd become a free agent at the age of seventeen. I was going to Montana to live with my father, she told me. There were no two ways about it, and this time I would not have the option of returning the next day. Originally, the travel plans didn't include my dog, but this time, knowing that I was leaving for good, I insisted that I be allowed to take Scotty, my four-year-old Sheltie. So Les bought a plastic crate big enough for the dog, and exactly a month after I'd come back, I was on a plane that first took me to Chicago, and then a smaller one that hopscotched across the Plains to Great Falls.

My father had driven to the airport in the white 1964 Ford pickup that his brother was lending him. It was a spartan vehicle without seat belts or power steering, made of steel and nothing but. It gave you the impression of something that would last for-ever. We put Scotty and his crate in the back along with my bags and got on the road that would take us to Fort Benton. Once we were away from the airport, the feeling of space was impressive. You could walk for days and never see anyone, and the houses we passed were like specks against the plateaus and fields of wheat on the horizon. It was all very different from Florida, and while I'd visited Montana before, I'd never seen this area of the state. You could get lost out here, I thought, and maybe that was just what Greg wanted.

It was the first time together since our meeting by the sea-wall, and as usual when he wasn't manic or depressed but some-where in between, he was a great guy to be with. I was a bit nervous and unsure of what to say, and he could tell. He knew that I had been told to come, and that I would have stayed with Les and Doris had I been given a choice. He tried to break the ice by asking me a few questions about the flight, and my dog, and when that didn't work, he started talking about the house he'd bought outside of town with a view of the Missouri River. As he put it, the idea behind his apparent show of settling down had been to entice Valerie to move out there with her children, but she hadn't taken his bait. She was still in New York, and he was living alone in the three-bedroom house, complete with a corral and a pony that he'd picked up for the kids.

I wasn't expecting anything in particular from the house. Greg was a doctor with additional income that came from his fa-ther's estate, and even if that hadn't been enough, banks all over the country would have fallen all over themselves to provide him with the credit he needed for a suitable house. He was a sure risk, which is to say that Greg could treat himself nicely when he wanted to. So the fact that the house I walked into was completely devoid of furniture was something of a surprise. It was absolutely bare, but had "potential," he told me, and the proof was the panoramic, double-thickness, thermal window that he'd had installed with a view of the duck pond. It had cost him $700, but it was worth every penny, he assured me.

"It keeps the heat in during the winter," he said, and I thought, great—while the rest of the house lets it out like a spaghetti strainer.

But where were the chairs, I wondered, and the beds? What were we going to sleep on? Looking around, I saw that there wasn't even a kitchen. There was a sink with running water, but no fridge and no oven.

"I usually have dinner at the hospital cafeteria," he said.

There was a toilet and a tub, so baths were possible, but there were no towels or soap. There was an electric razor on the sink, and a tube of toothpaste, but no toothbrush.

"Leave your stuff in one of the bedrooms," he said, "and we'll go have a look around outside." He wanted to show me the corral and the pony, but also the shed where his food was kept, and then the river.

"I haven't been here for too long," he told me as we walked around the side of the house to the corral. "Haven't really had a chance to set it up."

"It's a big house," I said, trying to sound upbeat. "Lots of room."

"Well, that was the idea," he said. "A place where there'd be room for all of us."

The brown-and-white pony trotted over to us from the other side of the corral. Its mane and tail were very long, and its forehead and half-hidden eyes made me think of an English sheepdog. The pony wanted some food, so my father handed it some hay from the ground.

"I haven't given it a name," he said. "The kids were gonna do that." When the pony finished eating, we continued down the path toward the water. There were poplars all around us; the color of the leaves was extraordinary, a kind of shimmering gold in the late-afternoon sun.

"It's nice, isn't it?" he asked, not really expecting an answer as we watched the flow of a river that had once guided explorers and settlers to another world.

Like his father before him, Greg was fascinated by the frontier and what it represented. The open spaces and the sense of freedom appealed to him, and just as cowboys would often take the law into their own hands, making up the rules as they went along, my father was also improvising, secretly living his life on the gender edge in a town that advertised itself as the "Birthplace of the Old West."

But more than the cowboys, Greg admired the Native Americans—not the present-day ones, but the historical ones, the nations that had fought the federal government in the late 1800s. He admired their spirit and damn-the-torpedoes attitude, their courage and their tragic end. They were losers, but with their shoulder-length hair or their Mohawks, they had a style that said "It's okay to be who you are." A postcard from a string of fourteen that he wrote to my girlfriend and me one afternoon when I was staying with him in Missoula shows how much he identified with these warriors. It was at the height of one of his manic phases, and in barely legible handwriting, he says to Ornella, "This is chief Plenty Coux [Coups]. Isn't he handsome and proud like your someday father?"

On another card that featured a group of cowhands, as immortalized in L. A. Huffman's photograph, "Waiting for the Irons to Heat," he wrote: "I treated the little fellow circled—his young daughter came 1,000 miles to see him when he was dying." It was from the period when he worked at another hospital in Jordan in the eastern part of the state. He would eventually spend almost ten years of his career in Montana. For most of that time I was away at university and we didn't see each other, but in the beginning, when he was just starting out in Fort Benton, we were together.

I could see that it was difficult for him to be the junior doctor in town. The job that he'd taken was mostly connected with the hospital, and didn't pay very much. The bulk of the town's private practice was solidly in the hands of the MD who had been there for years, and who showed no signs of wanting to retire. Being the intensely competitive person that he was, and very much like Ernest in this respect, his number-two status was a constant aggravation.

"I've just got the leftovers," he told me once as I picked up a jar containing a tapeworm in formaldehyde that he'd removed from one of his patients. We were in the tiny studio office that he'd rented in the center of town. There was a narrow, almost claustrophobic hallway where he kept his specimens and supplies, and an all-white room where people came to see him, sometimes walking in off the street without an appointment. There was no receptionist, not an office plant in sight—just a few chairs, a desk, a scale, and an examining table for the patients. It was very bare, and fit in with the stark quality that I'd come to associate with the state.

I was there for about two months, long enough to enroll in the local high school and to get a driver's license. The exam was easy even by American standards: twenty multiple-choice questions and then a driving test that took you around two city blocks, where there was never any traffic. You really had to be blind not to pass it, but when I finished and the examiner gave me my license, my dad was enormously relieved. He'd taken the afternoon off work and had walked back and forth between the hospital and his office, trying to shake the nervousness that he felt. He was worried silly that something would go wrong or that I'd get in an accident, and I remember thinking that I'd never seen him act this way before, fretting more like a mother than a father.

It was the first sign that he was slipping into a depression. The weather was changing and the short Montana summer was coming to an end. His moods were seasonal, and in the afternoons when I'd see him for dinner at the hospital cafeteria, he complained more and more about the other doctor in town, saying that at this rate, he'd never be making the kind of money he needed to make. I told him that he would, and that he just had to keep at it and everything would work out, but the black-ass pit of failure was there in front of him, and not even a two-day deer hunt could snap him out of his gathering gloom.

His friend Larry, who worked as a technician in the hospital, was fanatical about hunting, and the outdoors in general. I don't think he was from Montana (he might have been from Texas), but he loved the state, and I'm sure that his wife never saw him on weekends. A collector of guns and also a skilled bow hunter, Larry had gone with my dad to a store in Great Falls to help Greg choose the right weapon. Up till then, I'd never seen a compound bow with its double row of cords, cams, and fiberglass "limbs." The day before we left, Greg let me try it a few times so that I could get the hang of it. As a boy I had been very good at archery, but I'd never used anything like this. We set up a target on the road in front of the house, and when I pulled the cord back, I felt how easy it was to hold it. The seventy-pound bow had a let-off of twenty pounds at full stroke, which in layman's terms meant that you didn't need to strain like Hercules as you frantically aimed at a sometimes very spooked animal.

Showing me his new toy and the two cams that allowed you to hold it with such ease, Greg seemed to cheer up a bit. In 1977, it represented the cutting edge of bow-hunting technology and had cost him a good bit of money, which he was more than willing to spend. My father was like a kid in a toy store when he saw something that he liked. If he wasn't broke he'd buy it, but after the excitement had worn off, he'd just as often forget about it or give it away to the first person who reminded him what a nice bow, or canoe, or car he had. Material possessions had never meant much to him. They were prized only insofar as they were new or different.

Larry took us to an area where he was sure we'd find a lot of deer. We went in his car and packed enough food and beer for the two days, along with our sleeping bags and tents. The first night out was very cold. My father and I woke up freezing, but Larry was fine. He seemed to thrive in the bracing weather, and reminded us as he poured himself a cup of coffee that we didn't have much time.

"It's either now or at sunset," said Larry, as I laced up the hiking boots he'd loaned me. My fingers felt like sticks in the cold, and I thought about Miami and how it was two hours later there.

"Wouldn't it be easier," said my dad over the steam of his coffee, "if we just went to a supermarket and bought a couple of steaks?"

He'd buttoned up his down-filled vest, and looking at him, I noticed the flecks of gray in his hair. He said this made his patients trust him more. "People don't want a young doctor," he'd told me. "Inexperience kills." He was forty-five at the time, trim, with very strong arms—the part of his body, along with his eyes and smile, that I thought most resembled his father. They both had these massive arms, while mine were thin and gangly in comparison.

We walked the entire morning, but the deer must have known that we were coming; the one buck we did see was never close enough for a good shot. It was a tiring sport for a novice like me. I had this idea that it wouldn't take us long. We'd see a pair of antlers, shoot, and that would be that. But nine times out of ten in bow hunting, if you made too much noise, or were just plain unlucky, you went home empty-handed.

After a lunch break—where Larry chopped the head off a rattlesnake that had been foolish enough to seek a bit of heat near the spot where we were eating—we continued our hunt. We walked for miles, but there were no deer, and in the evening when we came back to our tents, my father decided that he'd had enough. In his mind nothing was going to work. Not the hunt, or the job, or any future reunion with his family. The depression was taking over, and even though I was getting used to living with him and had made some friends at the high school in Fort Benton, I knew that we would have to leave.

Back at the house he called his brother Pat in Bozeman and told him that he was quitting his job, and that we'd be there soon. I asked him what I was going to do with my dog, Scotty—if we could bring him with us—and he said that we couldn't. We were going back to New York, and there was no room in Valerie's apartment.

"Larry will take care of him," he told me. And that was how it ended—with my father and I driving away in the old Ford as Scotty ran after us to the end of the road, where he stopped and then waited. I never saw the dog again, but I heard that when Larry caught him and took him over to his house, Scotty escaped and ran back to the old place. He never left, hoping that some day I'd return.

We stayed in Bozeman for about a week, and it was the first time that I'd seen my uncle Patrick since 1971. He had a spare, unassuming house on the outskirts of town that was filled with books and Hemingway mementos, like the hunting rifle that had once been his father's, now hanging on the wall over the fireplace. I asked him how old it was, and he said that Ernest had used it in Africa in the 1950s. It was a gun that could easily fetch well over a $100,000 today, but unfortunately for my uncle, thieves broke into his house a few years later and stole it.

As far as I know, my dad didn't keep anything that had been his father's; or if he ever did, it was only for the time it took to give it away. He was about as different from his brother as you could get. Patrick was the responsible one, while Greg, the financial anarchist, was always running out of money and depending on Patrick to pick up the pieces when he'd fall. They were at psychologically opposite poles, and I remember a series of conversations they had in the living room of Patrick's house before we went back to New York. My uncle didn't want Greg to leave Montana, and was trying to convince him to stay.

Once I walked in when my father was telling Pat that he didn't want to die. He was looking pissed off at the thought that there was no way around the inevitable end. He was feeling sorry for himself, and Patrick told him that the best he could hope for was a kind of genetic immortality through his children. But for Greg, that wasn't good enough. He wasn't looking forward to the hereafter; he wanted to stick around. Patrick politely insisted that there wasn't much he could do. It was a one-way ticket, and what mattered was what you did now, how you lived your life.

"Bullshit," said Greg. He didn't want to die, but he also felt that there was nothing worth living for and no one worth helping, because everyone abandoned you in the end.

At which point I spoke up and said that I disagreed, that there *were* good people and that Uncle Les was one of them.

"Leicester?" said Patrick.

"I lived with him for four years, and I'd help him now if I could." Les wasn't struggling but he certainly wasn't rich and if there was one person who could use and who deserved a bit of the family's wealth it was him, but I don't think that either of them had a very high opinion of their uncle, and they seemed surprised by what I was saying.

"And what would you do?" asked Patrick.

"I'd send him some money." My uncle smiled. He must have been intrigued by this vein of generosity, because a few months later he decided to test my sincerity by offering me a $1,000 to use as I saw fit. I was at boarding school and got a phone call from Alfred Rice, the lawyer who'd worked for my grandfather and who was still managing the estate. He said that Patrick had given me the money and asked what I wanted to do with it. I told him that I didn't know, and wondered if there was anything that my uncle wanted me to do with it.

"No," said Rice, "your uncle Pat wants you to have this money, and there are no strings attached. It's up to you." At the time I had forgotten about the conversation in my uncle's living room, and I didn't see the connection with the money, but just the same I ended up giving half the amount to Les and Doris. Apparently by doing so, I proved my uncle Pat wrong and my stepmother right. According to Valerie, Patrick was betting that I'd keep the thousand, while Val was telling him, "No, you watch; he's a good boy. He'll help his uncle out."

The cynicism of my uncle's experiment was emblematic of a lot that wasn't right with the Hemingways, and a condition that has continued to this day with my family's commercial exploitation of Ernest's name and image. I never met my grandfather, but I sometimes wonder what he'd think to see his "essence" expressed in salad dressing, furniture, and wallpaper.

My father wasn't involved in Patrick's sincerity test. He had other things to worry about. The black-ass pit of his depression that had appeared in Fort Benton swallowed him whole in Bozeman, and three days after the living-room conversation, we were on a plane to New York.

Chapter 9

LOS ANGELES

While Los Angeles was a city that Ernest pretty much ignored—having none of the open spaces of Africa, the charm of Paris, or the mercurial blue of the Gulf Stream—it did play an important part in the life of his youngest son, and in mine. Like Greg I headed out West after I graduated from Canterbury School in Connecticut, and like my father, I studied at UCLA. During my junior year of high school, when I was applying to universities, my dad had suggested that I try out his quasi alma mater and see if I got lucky. Paying next to nothing in the 1950s for him had been a great deal, but it was still a bargain in 1979 compared to what you'd spend at any Ivy League university. Greg liked the idea of a good, low-cost, public education, but also liked that I was following in his footsteps. First at his prep school, and then off to UCLA—but not exactly. With my father, nothing was ever that simple.

What brought Greg to Los Angeles was not a BA from the U.C. system, but Dianetics. In 1950 he was studying psychology and undergoing therapy at the Hubbard Dianetics Research Foundation in Elizabeth, New Jersey. In a letter written to his father on July 15, he apologizes for not going down to Cuba that summer, but says that his work at the foundation was very interesting, and that if Ernest didn't mind, he'd like to keep at it. He had, with his fellow researchers, found nothing less than "the answer to insanity and organic psychosomatic disorders." He told his father that he wouldn't say something like this unless he was absolutely sure, and he was. "I've seen it; it works," he assured him. But to really get Papa's interest, he talks about an illness that Ernest was always mentioning in his letters.

> Dianetics has proven high blood pressure to be psychosomatic in origin and can cure it. That buzzing in your ears which Stelky on his tube calls a "delusion" has been proven to be the result of pain received while you were inside your mother's womb (which has been proven to be far from the paradise Freud thought it was). And the buzzing was probably the effect caused by the pain and unconsciousness which your mother's high blood pressure produced when you were an embryo. It has been proven that the zygotic embryo and foetus record on a cellular level stimuli received during moments of pain or unconsciousness. Example: two months after conception, mother bumps into a table and knocks the embryo "unconscious." Now anything that mother or anyone else around the child says during this period of unconsciousness is recorded as a destructive and permanent impression on the protoplasm of the cell. What was said during this time can be recalled in later life by the patient.[22]

He then adds (and I can just imagine how relieved Ernest must have felt to read this) that all of this is impossible for his father to understand completely, because it would take him at least five pages to explain it; but that this was just to 'wet' his curiosity."

In another letter dated December 7, he says that his girlfriend's father, the publisher of L. Ron Hubbard and his Dianetics texts, wants to visit Ernest in Cuba, and is going to send him one of Hubbard's latest works.

Ernest probably didn't think much of Hubbard and his crackpot science. On December 14, he wrote:

Dear Gig:

Thanks for the letter. Certainly hope your secretary can sing. The Dianetics king never sent the book so I bought one, but Miss Nita borrowed it and it is still outside of the joint. So have not been able to practice jumping back into the womb or any of those popular New York indoor sports and have to just continue to write them as I see them.[23]

In January of 1951 the real Dianetics King, L. Ron Hubbard himself, told Greg and a friend to pack all of their personal possessions and drive out to Los Angeles. The New Jersey Board of Medical Examiners had instituted proceedings against Hubbard for teaching medicine without a license, and the cult leader had decided that it was time to move to a state where his genius would be duly appreciated.[24]

Greg hung around Hubbard and the Dianetics crowd for most of the period that he was in Los Angeles, even if by the end of 1950 he was already writing to his father that he'd begun to have his doubts about its actual effectiveness in curing what ailed him. Ernest was telling his son that if, in fact, he wanted to study medicine, then he should get serious about it and apply to a legit school. When I was with Uncle Les, he once mentioned Greg and his Dianetics period, telling me how my father had stayed with Hubbard and his second wife, Sara, and how Ernest thought that the whole thing was pretty loony and yet another example of "Gigi's" bad judgment.

Hubbard was perhaps one of the greatest American con artists who ever lived, and if my grandfather had been aware of even a quarter of what was going on—if he'd known how the Dianetics dictator had kidnapped his own one-year-old daughter in an effort to prove his wife insane because he wanted to dump her and then settle in with his new lover, or how Hubbard would denounce those who spoke out against him to the FBI as communists—I'm sure that Ernest would have caught the next plane out to LA to forcefully drag his son back to Havana.

On the other hand, I can sympathize with my father's predicament. He was only nineteen, and desperate for a way to control what he sometimes referred to in his letters to Ernest as his "degeneration." His cross-dressing, by his own admission, was beyond his control, and he turned to Dianetics in a misguided attempt to get a grip on the devil that tormented him. Certainly he wasn't the only one to be duped by Hubbard. At $500 for a full course, a complete "audit" of one's subconscious, thousands of gullible people were sending in their checks. By the early 1950s, Hubbard was already boasting that he was raking in the salary of Clark Gable.[25]

In December of 1950, Greg was classified 1-A for the draft and fully expected to be called up by February. He didn't want to fight in Korea, and while he later wrote in a letter to Ernest that his sudden marriage to Jane Rhodes was the "logical thing to do if we were going to have a child"[26] (she was pregnant with my sister Lorian), it certainly couldn't have hurt him when it came to steering clear of the war. He was now married and a father-to-be. The army would leave him alone.

While technically a minor until the age of twenty-one and in need of parental approval to marry, Greg tied the knot without his father's approval at the age of nineteen. His mother Pauline and her sister Jinny were in on the big decision, but Ernest was told only after it was a *fait accompli*. He was not amused. In a cable from April 30, 1951, he wrote:

> Have received no letters from you since you left here in January stop give absolutely no consent nor approval to your marriage without full details and opportunity to check stop love Papa.[27]

In the same letter where he said that it was "the logical thing to do" (written the day after his marriage), Greg describes Jane as "a wonderful girl, and I know you will love her. She has all the sensitivity and what you call class, which both Puck and Henry lack. And she is one of the most beautiful women I have ever met (really!). Mother was crazy about her and so was Aunt Jinny, although I am afraid that this may not be of much comfort to you." Greg writes that of course Ernest will have to meet her and see for himself what a beauty she is, but that this probably wouldn't happen before Christmas, as both of them were working at Douglas Aircraft and the baby was due in December. He finishes off the letter with an apology of sorts, saying, "I am terribly hurt that I didn't let you know earlier, but am sure that I made the right decision and know that this is the chief cause of your concern."[28]

Greg's teenage wedding was certainly an impulsive act, but it was also romantic, and I can't help but think that the man who was famous for having written some of the world's greatest love stories didn't in some way secretly approve.

Ernest wrote to his son again on May 2, 1951, reiterating that he wasn't at all happy about the way "this business," as he called it, had been dealt with, blaming in equal parts Greg, Pauline, and her sister Jinny. He then added:

Also, as an aid to your conduct in life, write your father and your good friends when you are not in trouble and do not need anything. That way they appreciate the ill-spelled, un-grammatical, in-trouble letters better.

And FOR CHRIST SWEET SAKE, learn to write a decent, grammatical, comparatively properly spelled letter whether you are in, or out of trouble.

I know I spell and write badly; but I have earned the right not to. You haven't.[29]

Greg didn't take it personally. He must have been accustomed to his dad's criticism, and communication between the two of them continued, although by the beginning of June, Ernest was clearly depressed. In a phone conversation, Ernest tells Greg that the financial situation is terrible, and Greg tries to cheer him up by saying that there must be a lighter side to Cuba.

. . . as there are still people and cats you can talk [to] and have fun with, aren't there? Or is the pit so black and deep that you can never extract yourself from it, even for a moment? That doesn't sound like you, Papa! No jolly times at all anymore? No! My pit is of course much smaller but seems to hold me quite adequately, and if I hear nothing from you but bad times, I might very soon come to think the world is nothing but a collection of black pits, and that would be bad indeed.[30]

He then fills Ernest in on the latest details of his financial situation so that Ernest wouldn't have to worry about it, or the possibility of going further into debt because of his son. What follows is a typical list of expenses and estimates that were often found in their letters to each other: maternity expenses for Lorian's birth

($300); a used car ($475); and then the money that they were using to pay for dental visits. All of which would be covered by Greg's weekly salary of $65, and the $100 a month that Ernest was sending to Pauline for Greg's support.

Ernest may have wanted a different kind of correspondence, something other than the "in-trouble" letters Greg would write to him when he was in school—but he couldn't expect to have it both ways, even if he was a literary icon. He had always been very careful with his expenses and exacting in his lists. Greg understood that this was the way you had to write to Papa, creating a mix of family information, accounting, weather, politics, and whatever else got thrown into the pot. I don't think there was anything mercenary or disrespectful in what they did; it was just their way of dealing with each other.

After Ernest's father's suicide, it was up to Ernest to sort out the mess of Clarence's finances, and he may have seen his father's financial insolvency and bad investments as an expression of the weakness that eventually killed him. Money problems had nothing to do with Clarence's clinical depression, but Ernest continued to compile his lists.

Greg wasn't at all like his father. He never managed to save much, but then, he didn't have to. When Ernest had money and one of his sons was in need, he didn't hesitate to dish it out. He might get uptight about his cash flow, bitch about his taxes or the "Pfeiffer blood money" that was sucking him dry with the IRS, but he was never miserly.

Pauline's death changed Greg's life enormously. As he wrote in his memoir, ". . . from being a poor aircraft mechanic struggling to support a wife and a child, I was suddenly a rich young man, having inherited a small fortune from my mother."[31] The money would still be controlled by his father until he was twenty-one, but he could now quit his job as a mechanic and indulge in all of the activities that he'd only been able to dream about before. He took flying lessons, writing about them enthusiastically to his father, and before the baby was born, he and Jane visited Ernest and Mary in Havana. Like most women meeting my grandfather for the first time, Jane was immediately won over by Ernest's sheer presence and charm. Once back in LA, Greg wrote to his father that Jane couldn't wait to see him again. More letters followed, filled with the usual mixture of money matters and family news.

When a deal with a prospective buyer for the old Key West house fell through, Greg's older brother Patrick recommends renting it. Ernest then asks Greg about his opinion on the matter, and when Greg doesn't get back to him, he writes:

> Have heard nothing from you in reply to my letters about Key West property situation (although Patrick on the phone told me that whatever we decided on that was O.K. with you according to his telephonic conversation with you). Have heard nothing either since I wrote you in reply to your letter about Pickett Land Company or have had any acknowledgement [sic] of checks sent.
>
> This type of letter probably bores the shit out of you, but it certainly bores the shit out of me to have to write it. Charlie Scribner died a week ago Monday and so it will be rather difficult for me to borrow money from him against my loan account paying 2% to send you a monthly check until you attain the age of 21 years. However, I will continue to send you this check unless I hear from you that you do not need it for your support. I will not go into a discussion of any economic difficulties but I would like you to write promptly to communications about money matters.
>
> Best love to you and your family.[32]

Greg then replies on the bottom half of his father's letter:

"I am not only tired of this type of letter but offended by every-one [everything] you write. If you were a shit as this type of letter would lead anyone to believe, I wouldn't mind, but I don't think you are and I love you very much and this is why I am offended.

Yes, you can stop sending the money if you want to."

Greg also reminds Ernest of a conversation they had regarding support checks:

> ... that went something like this, "O.K., Pal, I know I have more money than you do".
>
> I then said that I supported your legal obligation to pay the money [which] ended with mother's death. You said then that you didn't care about any legal obligation; you still had a moral obligation to pay the money. What has happened to that moral obligation now?[33]

Probably still very upset over the death of his publisher, Charles Scribner, and not overly disposed to accepting his son's criticism, Ernest sent the following letter on March 2:

> Dear Gig:
>
> Your letter of February 26th asking me "What has hap-pened to that moral obligation now?" must have crossed my letter written and mailed Feb. 29th encloseing [sic] a check for $100 for support for the month of March and your share of the net rent from Key West property which Patrick writes me he sent to me to forward to you.
>
> For your information I never took or received a dime from my family from the time I was 16. I paid my father's debts and supported various relatives and have supported Mary's father and mother since we were married. I do not

relish being called a shit by any teenage delinquent at the safe distance of several thousand miles, nor being questioned as to "What has happened to that moral obligation now?" when I wrote you asking whether you needed $100 a month Charlie Scribner had been sending and saying that I would send it gladly if you needed it.

Evidently the effort required to write a letter is so great in your present pathologic condition that you have to justify your sloppiness by attacking your best friends as an excuse for not being able to behave as a man. The deterioration in your handwriting and your spelling is a very alarming symtom [sic] of your condition.[34]

Ernest must have regretted writing what he did, because on March 9, he tells Greg not to worry if he doesn't hear from him for a couple of weeks. He was going to be on vacation. It had not been a very good period for Ernest, and he asked Greg if he knew that Colonel Cooper had died suddenly in Tanganyika. "I feel plenty bad about it, he and Blickie both gone and Wolfie listed as Believed Married the old gang is about wiped out.

Clara, the maid, finally made suicide on her 4th official try."

He mentions the mango trees that were in heavy bloom, and a product invented by Jose Luis based on the leaves of olive trees "that is probably going to be the non-harmful way for lowering hypertension." He ends the letter with a postscript about his deceased publisher.

Charlie Scribner dying so suddenly made things pretty complicated . . . We had our arguments but were good sound friends and understood each other. He was as much a friend as a publisher and his death made me very sad. I was trying to skip burdening you with any of this when I wrote you that I would omit personal problems or whatever the phrase was.

Have been busy trying to work them out and I have them
worked out so that there is money for your hundred dollars
a month until you are 21. So please never worry about that.[35]

In his book, *Papa: A Personal Memoir,* Greg says that the bad
blood between himself and his father began when he took Jane
and Lorian down to Cuba for a visit. As they were leaving, Ernest
said that it was his son's arrest for drug abuse (in reality, for cross-
dressing) that had killed Pauline. Greg writes: "Whatever his mo-
tives were, the yellow-green filter came back down over my eyes
and this time it didn't go away for seven years. I didn't say anything back to him. He'd almost always been right about things, he
was so sound, I knew he loved me, it must have been something
he just had to say, and I believed him."[36]

But in fact, the yellow-green filter didn't last for seven years. The
seriously nasty letters didn't even start until the end of 1952, almost
a year later, and Ernest was always in touch, if for no other reason
than to send him checks. He did blame Greg for his mother's death,
but not, as my father writes, during his visit to Cuba. It was the day
after Pauline died when Greg phoned him from Los Angeles. The
reasons behind their rift had as much to do with Greg's cross-
dressing and the embarrassment that both of them felt toward their
transvestic tendencies as it did with Pauline's death. To get a better
picture of what really happened, you have to look at the letters.

On July 3, when Greg writes to tell his father that he's finishing his exams at UCLA and that he wants to visit his older brother
Jack at Fort Bragg, his last words are for Mary:

> Give my love to Miss Mary and tell her if I see her again I
> sure as hell would like all to be forgiven. I did a terrible
> thing in lying about that clothes business and I make no
> excuses for it (except to say that the whole business is my

least rational aspect) but everyone's life is not simon says, I'm sure, and I used to like her a hell of a lot.[37]

Greg had stolen some of Mary's clothes and then accused one of the maids of the theft when Mary asked what had happened to them. Ernest doesn't appear to have taken it too seriously, even though he was the one who'd discovered his son's subterfuge, and I doubt that Mary—considering the kind of hair-dyeing missives and gender experiments that were going on between her and her husband—could have really thought it such a grave offense. She was angry, but it was Greg who was worried, because it was embarrassing and something that he couldn't help, and because it was, as Ernest had cruelly reminded him, intimately tied to the events that had led to his mother's death.

Three months passed, and the communication between the two continued amicably enough, with the usual mix of money matters and general information—what they called "gen"—on friends and family. On October 19, Greg said that they should sell the house in Key West, and that his schoolwork was improving.

> . . . and, wonders of wonders, I may have something to show for all this psychoanalysis soon. Wrote Bum [Jack] a letter but I guess he is much too important an Army man to answer his brother. (Horn sounds and bitter Hamlet leaves the stage.)
>
> Reviews of the Old Man have been 98% favorable and they are even praising it here at college as the first "Classical Tragedy" since Racine. Hem's stuffed Marlin penetrates intellectual lamp and Homer's or the Run. Extra.
>
> It's a damn good story, Papa.
>
> Much love,
> Gig[38]

Ernest must have answered with something that Greg didn't like, because in his next letter, Greg wrote: "You ever write another letter like that and I'll beat the shit out of you." I haven't found the letter that Ernest wrote, and can't say exactly what his words were (it had something to do with my Uncle Jack), but whatever it was set off a flood of anger in my father:

> How can you tell such bare-faced lies and make such un-founded accusations? You know Bum didn't write for the simple reason that Bum just doesn't write. Not a terrible fault at any means but not one to be excused on the grounds that he is one of our heros in kaiki [khaki] and that anything a man does or doesn't while in the Army is alright as long as he discharges his official duties properly, a philosophy that you have hid behind for innumerable wars.

Then, referring to Pauline, Greg says,

> When Mother died and I first called, you accused me of killing her. When I brought Jane down to Cuba you be-haved so inhumanly that after the trip was over I had to [. . .] myself for three whole days to stop myself from crying. I know you thought you were doing this all for my own good, but I hate the way you did it . . . As far as I'm concerned you can go to hell. If you want answers to any letter to me, make your own truthful and devoid of the epistles to the Californian shit . . . If we see each other again and you act nastily, I will fight and I will beat the shit out of you.[39]

Ten days later he wrote another letter to his father, and here he begins to list the things that he finds abusive in Ernest's character."

I used to think that you were such a wonderful guy in the mornings when your head was clear that whatever stupid, inane, illogical, ruthless and (to use your own word) Chicken-shit things you said later on in the day were excusable, and even must be sensible because they were coming out of the same person who could be so human and sensitive in the morning. Well, old boy, I'm sick of adding it all up—trying to balance things in your favor. Let me name a few things I'm tired of. 1) your incessant castigation of Marty, who was the second-best wife you ever had (after Bumby's mother). If ever there was a girl who was alive and with a capacity for enjoying things, it was Marty. She never bitched you without reason, never bitched you until you had made a thousand and one tantramental [sic] scenes, made her so sick of you and so destroyed her love for you that she was delighted to leave you finally; and now she lives a peaceful (but duller) life in Mexico where she no longer has to fare [sic] an illogical, torpid bull every evening.

That is the big decision everyone who is close to you has to make eventually—whether to stick and live for the few times when you are kind, perceptive and human (and by sticking and waiting for these times they undervaluate themselves and forget that in their own way they are twice as good as you), or to leave and be rid of this gin-soaked, abusive monster.

When it's all added up, papa it will be: he wrote a few good stories, had a novel and fresh approach to reality and he destroyed five persons—Hadley, Pauline, Marty, Patrick, and possibly myself. Which do you think is the most important, your self-centered shit, the stories or the people? I shouldn't say destroyed; some are getting over you—Mouse for one. Hadley completely recovered. Marty is her old self and a little wiser, I hope. Mother is dead, but before she died she was pretty free. God damn you for the things you did to her. She told me that when she met your boat when you came home from the Spanish war, you were drunk, and when she put her arms around you, you brushed by her and went ahead to take care of your luggage. You accused me of killing her—said it was my arrest that killed her. For your information, a heart condition is incurred over a period of time. Do you think that little scene did her any good? I would never think of accusing you of killing her—I think I have too good an understanding of the scope of this business we call life—but you accused me, you cocksucker— you wonder if I don't forget all and kiss your sickly ass when you send me a birthday greeting? You think you can repair a break in a dam with a telegram? God have mercy on your soul for the misery you have caused. If I ever meet you again and you start pulling the ruthless, illogical and destructive shit on me, I will beat your head into the ground and mix it with cement to make outhouses. I don't expect you to take kindly to this letter. I can see your reaction now—Gig has gone crazy. You will never look toward yourself and wonder if you are at fault. But of the question— "Gig must be destroyed in my mind" you will think of all the horrible things I have ever done and will use them to convince yourself and the sychophants [sic] around you that I never really was any good—how you were mistaken but now you realize and oh, how you were fooled. Exactly the same process you went through with Marty. I know it well, papa, and you are welcome to it.

Gregory (over)

His postscript was almost as long as the letter itself:

P.S. Who is Rudy Davis?

And give my love to Gianfranco. An Amazing person—a sensitive man who can live with you and tolerate you.

Mouse can't. Hates you and loves you and stays away. But stays away. Last time he was here he told me he wasn't afraid of you. He colored, his voice became a little fanatical, and he said, "If I get in the same room with him he can never catch me. I can run around and he can never reach me, never catch me." Is this a loving attitude?

I can remember Bum the last time we were at Sun Valley. After that long talk in the living room of the MacDonald cabin, he came out and said, "I just won't take it anymore." "It" meaning your domineering attitude toward the way he ran his life. He was tense, the muscles on his face were jumping and you could see he was having a hard time controlling himself.

And poor old Mary, your present whipping post. Because of the truly terrible way that you treat her, she would have left you long ago but she's too old now—couldn't make her way in the newspaper world anymore—you have to sleep with people to get the important stories, you know. It would be pretty hard going now for her, so she sticks it out with you. She has told me this herself. Ask her; she may not be too smart, but Mary is honest, and you can always count on that. I realize a lot of confidences are being broken by me in this, but with something as destructive as you confidences have to be broken—the air must be cleared! You will die unmourned and basically unwanted unless you change, papa.

I guess you really never will change. You've had too much success and have blown yourself up too much in your own eyes to even think about change. But change toward me, you bastard. I won't accept the party line anymore. It makes sense or it's disregarded, as far as I'm concerned. All this is the truth and I know it will hurt and you will dismiss me from your mind but maybe your mind will be better off. I think I've been a thorn in your conscience for a long time.[40]

Without waiting for a reply he wrote again the next day. The floodgates had been opened and he had years of catching up to do.

I suppose you wonder what has happened to all my filial respect for you. Well, it's gone, Ernestine, dear, it's gone! It's gone with the hundred thousand cruelties you have inflicted on people for the last ten years and with the thousand righteous drunks of that period. You kept me under thumb very subtlely, broke my spirit, and while I stood by in wondrous amazement at my tutor, [he] proceeded to get drunker and drunker, making a mockery of good fellowship and decency and all the while praising yourself—telling the boys how you needed cases of champagne in order to produce the wonderful books that everybody loved—that every body sat around breathlessly waiting for. (When will he write the great novel, will it be that long one he's been working on for ten years—HA!) Well, that's alright for the sycophants who surround you. Little goody-goody Miss Mary, for instance, who's taken more shit from you than they dump in Havana harbor. But we know better, don't we, you'll never write that great novel because you're a sick man—sick in the head and too fucking proud and scared to admit it. In spite of the critics, that last one was as sickly a bucket of sentimental slop as was ever scrubbed off a barroom floor. There's nothing I'd rather see than you write a beauty and there's nothing I'd rather see than you act intelligently, but until you do I'm going to give you just what you deserve, and in extra large handfuls to make up for the trouble you've caused me.[41]

Reading these letters, I was sincerely surprised at their intensity. I've known for a long time that Greg probably hated Ernest as much as he loved him, but these words brought home the reality of that conflict. While I think that my father was being honest in describing the difficulties of living with Ernest, I also believe that nobody's perfect; I don't know how I would have reacted in my grandfather's shoes. Were my own son to write to me and repeat what Greg said to my grandfather, I know that I'd be angry, but at the same time very sad, especially if I knew that much of what he was saying was true. It's one of those situations where you're damned if you do and damned if you don't. You can't keep quiet and you can't speak out. Either way, someone is going to get hurt.

Ernest's answer was prompt and to the point. He wanted a written apology to Mary and wanted one as soon as possible.

. . . You stole from Mary, you may remember, and now you write obscenely and insultingly about her.

Your threats to beat up your father are comic enough. Ordinarily I would ignore such nonsense. But obscene threatening letters sent through the United States mails are not comic at all.

Your letter of November 13th was sent after you had received a cable of congratulation for your twenty-first birthday by your friends and well wishers here. You ask who is Rudy Davis? He is a shooter that you evidently do not remember.

You shot against him many times when he was a beginner. He has now become a very fine shooter and this year ran 116 straight at skeet. We happened to run into him and his wife the night before your birthday. He is a great admirer of yours.

I had received your previous letter before your birthday. But I remembered how you had nearly always been away from home on your birthday, and so it had been neglected as a fiesta. Since your 21st was a very special birthday, I thought you would like to hear from people who were fond of you and wished you well.

I would like to see you straighten up and fly right.

Mary has been very patient with you. The night before your obscene threatening letter came, we had been awake late in bed and she had been reading the journal she kept of a trip we made, and we were remembering places, and the colours of things, and the fine times we had. Then in the morning with the breakfast mail your letter came. It was as pleasant and charming and as decent as a dead buzzard, and about as popular. In some ways a dead buzzard is comic. In some ways the letter was comic. But it was Chatahoochee [sic] Choo-Choo comic, and that is the sort of comic you want to avoid. That's the train to keep off of.

Straighten up and fly right, Gig. I have learned from your letters, if I did not know it before, that I am not always a charming character. But I am not a gin-soaked monster going around ruining people's lives and all my friends are not sychophants [sic] (You spell it). George Brown is not, Charlie Sweeny is not, Sinsky, Ermua and Patxchi are not, Buck Lanham is not, Mr. Sully is not, Mary is not, Taylor Williams is not, Mike Burke is not, Mike Ward is not, Red Pelky is not, Coops is not, Chuck Atkinson and Purdy are not, nor is Lou Hill, nor is Mon Wogaman, nor Chub

Weaver, nor Kid Tunero, nor Gianfranco, nor John Lough-
ney, Philip Percival is not. Archie Crabbe could be hardly so
described. Cheer up, pal, and don't dump anymore dead
buzzard letters with people's breakfast mail. People like you
[who] have never had to accept any discipline except the time
clock are apt to think that their integrities and personalities
etc. are being violated when they are bawled out for their
own good. In this letter you are not being bawled out at all.

You are being asked to write a prompt apology to Mary,
and you are being asked not to write me any more letters
unless they are necessary business letters. In that case
write them clearly and on a typewriter. Your handwriting is
ill formed and illegible. When you have time on your
hands you might work on that. It has shown a progressive
degeneration since you left prep-school. Sometimes the degeneration in it has been shocking.

But I wish you all luck. If your hand-writing improves
you will probably be improving.

Your mother wrote me before she died that she did not
believe that you were taking drugs but that you had simply
deteriorated mentally so that you were unable to accept any
discipline and that even any suggestions angered you. But
she said that you still had flashes of your old charm and decency and that we should never give up hope that you
would come through whatever was happening to you.
Right now I could use a good flash of your old charm and
decency. I cannot use any more obscene or threatening letters. Mary can do without your thefts and your insults. But
at present it is necessary to send her, promptly, a letter of
apology for your letter of November 13th.

Sin mas nada

Your father, E. Hemingway[42]

Greg wrote back to Ernest that he had no apologies to make. He admitted that he had called Mary a "goody-goody," but that sometimes she was one. He wrote that neither she nor Ernest was perfect, and that he had just as much a right to criticize them when he thought they deserved it. He said that he was painfully hurt by Mary's reaction to Ernest's discovery that Greg had lied about the clothes.

> The clothes business is something that I have never been able to control, understand basically very little, and I am terribly ashamed of. I have lied about it before, mainly to people I am fond of, because I was afraid they would not like me as much if they found out. It has been a terribly destructive influence on my life and is undoubtedly responsible for a lot of moral disintegration. I was very hurt by the cold way she treated me when I was done [sic] there with Jane. Well, that's O.K., maybe I deserved it. But I want you two to realize that you are not Gods . . . No apologies, Miss Mary, but a lot of love to you.[43]

He finished by telling his father that he didn't want to be ordered around anymore, but that he still had a lot to love him for, and that maybe this would eventually bring them back together again. Greg needed his own space, and Ernest did nothing to stop him. He knew how stubborn his son could be.

Just like his old man.

Chapter 10

REWRITING THE PAST

I must have been about five the first time my father ever told me about Africa. We were still living in the house on Mary Street in Coconut Grove and Greg had organized a safari with some fellow interns. When he left I remember thinking that he was away for a long time but it probably wasn't more than a couple of weeks. The day he came back was a surprise. A cab dropped him off in front of the house and he looked very tanned and fit as he told me about the animals that he'd hunted and how he'd lived in a tent with his friends in an open field. I was very impressed and tried to picture him with a rifle and safari hat on a plain that in my mind looked more like our back yard than the Serengeti. It wasn't the first time that he'd been to Africa, but when I was a boy he hardly ever talked about his life before he met my mother.

My father had a talent for whiting out periods of his life, so that whole sections of his past could disappear through omission. For instance, in his memoir, *Papa,* his marriage to my mother is never mentioned; it's as if it never happened. The reader is conveniently taken from the end of the first marriage to the beginning of the third. He meets Valerie at his father's funeral, they get hitched a few years later, and everyone lived happily ever after. Nothing was ever said of my parents' breakup or how that happened, or how they met, or even what Greg was doing after he left Jane. In this revised personal history, he wanted to show everyone how different he was from Ernest, and to do that, many of the messier aspects of his life had to be cut out.

On page nine of his memoir, Greg says that when his father's plane crashed in Africa in 1954 and no one had any news from him, he thought that Ernest was dead. It was then that Greg realized how much he loved him. When the world later discovered that the great writer was still alive, Greg decided it was time to put aside their differences and make amends.[44]

But of course, in his book, he doesn't mention the letter from the beginning of May 1954. It was the one where he apologized, saying he was sorry for what he'd written in "those letters" from October of 1952: "I didn't mean to say those things. I was crazy at the time, just as crazy as Mouse was when he used to swing at you during the shock treatments. If you don't ever want to see me again, O.K., but I hope you will change your mind when you find out over a period of time that I am on my feet again."[45]

Reading this reminded me of my own need to make amends with Greg, and of a letter I'd sent him in 1999 after a break that had lasted nearly ten years. I remember that I apologized for the argument that we'd had, and for the harsh words, saying that I was under a lot of stress. While there was no excuse for my cutting him off, I hoped that he would forgive me. He did, of course, because he was a generous man who, like his father, loved all his children, but also because I reminded him of his own past.

Ernest wasn't one to keep a grudge with his youngest son, and soon their letters were back on a more even footing. Not just business, but also plans and "gen" (general information) about the family and friends. Greg was going to apply to UCLA med school, and Pat was working in Tanganyika. They talked a lot about Africa, and it wasn't long before Greg decided that he couldn't miss out on the family obsession. Plans were made, and Ernest promised to loan him money for the trip. Greg estimated that the total cost would hover around $3,000, and initially the idea was to get that money from the sale of some of Ernest's original manuscripts. Technically, however, they didn't belong to him, but to his two sons, my father and my uncle Patrick, who had inherited them from their great-uncle, Gus Pfeiffer. My grandfather and Pauline's uncle Gus had been quite close, and Ernest had given him several of his works over the years. In a letter to Patrick and Greg from the executors of his estate, the manuscripts were listed as follows:

> For Whom the Bell Tolls
> A Farewell to Arms
> Fifty Grand (Original manuscript of an unpublished portion)
> The Killers
> The Undefeated (First typescript)
> Lion Hunting
> Notes on Dangerous Game
>
> The estimated value of the manuscripts is around $25,000.[46]

It was a sizeable sum for the period, and in a letter dated September 20, 1954, Greg writes about the importance of making reservations in advance.

> You mentioned that we might come down to Cuba to see you this winter, or go over to Africa to see Mouse if you

were able to realize some dough from the sale of a manuscript. Why shouldn't we do both? . . . [W]e could come straight to Cuba, stay a couple of weeks with you, and then take that boat from Havana that you took—or some other line like it. I would love to do it and would like to go ahead with all plans just as if we knew for certain you could make the sale, that is, write for passports (I've already done this!), make reservations, get everything in order. Then if you can sell a manuscript and we can get a little dough, wonderful; if not, better luck next time, Mr. Chips!

He said that he wasn't trying to push Ernest into making a hasty sale, nor had he handed over the manuscripts with the idea of getting "some sort of gift."

I did it simply because the manuscripts are yours and I expected nothing from it. But who, alas, am I to turn down a free trip to Africa from one so rich and generous. (that's a great line, worthy of young Darmon Bunyon or, perhaps, Worthless Weechee.)[47]

Two weeks later Greg confirmed sending the manuscripts, and gave an item-by-item breakdown of the cost of the Africa trip. The total had now been reduced to $2,500, including Lorian's expenses and half of Ada Stern's fare. His former governess was now looking after his daughter, and while she'd been a difficult substitute mother for Greg, he didn't hold anything against her. Quite the contrary.

"You might ask why take Ada," Greg writes to his father. "I owe her a lot. She took care of me until I was twelve, was practically my mother. She's sixty-seven now and got the burnt end of the stick all her life. I'd like to give her something before she

Ernest's parents, Clarence and Grace Hall Hemingway

Ernest as toddler dressed in girls' clothes.

Leicester, 2, dressed as a girl with comment on left-hand side written by his mother, Grace.

Pauline Hemingway and son Greg leaving Pan Am seaplane on a tender for shore, Bimini, 1935.

Jane Mason and Pauline Hemingway standing near a shark on Bimini dock, 1935.

Pauline, Gregory, Ernest, John (Jack), and Patrick, Bimini, 1935.

Leicester and Ernest with Martha Gelhorn on Leicester's sailboat, Havana, 1940s.

Ernest with sons Patrick, John, and Gregory, Cuba, 1947.

Greg, about 8 or 9, playing baseball, Cuba.

*Greg and tribal
girl, at the end
of the film
he made in
Angola, 1959.*

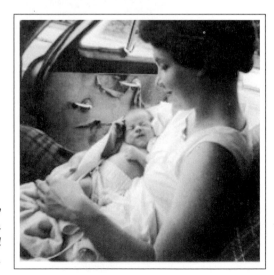

*Alice Thomas Hemingway
with newborn son, John
Hemingway, Miami, end
of August, 1960.*

John with Doris, Anne, Hilary, and Leicester Hemingway, Miami Beach house, 1976.

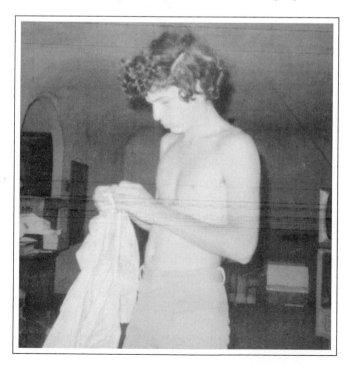

*John
Hemingway
in Leicester
Hemingway's
Miami Beach
house, 1976.*

Photo of Gregory Hemingway and his wife, Ida Mae Galliher, at the grand opening of the Hemingway-Pfeiffer Museum and Educational Center in Pigott, Arkansas, July 4, 1999. Photo courtesy of the Jonesboro Sun.

Police photo of Gregory Hemingway taken at the Miami-Dade County Women's Detention Facility on September 26th, 2001, when he was booked on charges of indecent exposure.

dies."[48] In three letters that he wrote on October 12, 13, and 19, Ernest did his level best to dissuade his youngest son from taking Lorian and Ada. He felt that the disadvantages far outweighed the advantages, and Ernest didn't hesitate in listing them.

When I first wrote you I thought that just you and Jane would be going. That is simple. Making this very long trip with an infant daughter and a 68-year-old [sic] nurse is complicated and tiring and wearing and it is an awfully good bet that long before you reach Mouse's you will wish you had never undertaken it. This is just general gen. Will get back to the staffing out part. Gig, you don't know how Ada will stand up to a trip like this. You could very easily lose her on the trip. With the best will and courage in the world things can be too much for people.

If you spoke Swahili it would be a lot easier. But watching your daughter's food, water, taking proper precautions against malaria, black-water, both sorts of dysentery etc. for a young child is a full-time job, and if you should have Ada sick at the same time it could be awful. It is very healthy where Mouse lives, cool at nights, beautiful in the daytime and with no fever. But on the Great North road, which is the only way you can reach him except by flying, you go through really bad fever patches and some bad tsetse fly country. Honest to God, Gig, if I had a daughter the age of yours, I would not take her out there now, especially under present conditions. First of all, there are all the inoculations which are often very hard on kids. You must have typhoid, paratyphoid, typhus, cholera, yellow fever and smallpox inoculations, and an international certificate of vaccination book for all of them for each individual. This you mustn't lose or you will have to take them all again. The Yellow Fever inoculation made even me sick.

These all might raise the devil with Ada too. Then you must take your Paludrine tablets every day (and a week before landing in Mombassa) if you are not to get Malaria. This you have to do absolutely without fail. Patrick picked up a bad case of Malaria coming up the Great North road to hunt with us in a wonderful country in Kenya. Henny was ill and he had to fly down to Iringa to the hospital where she was, and while he was there his fever came on and he lost out on his hunting trip which was starting wonderfully. He had been living in his own healthy country where you do not need to take precautions and the malaria nailed him as he camped in a bad fever country.

Gig, I honestly do not think that you should take Lorian and Ada to Africa. If you and Jane go, you are a movable unit for what transport Patrick has, and you can take it the rough way and enjoy it. You will see the country and have a wonderful time and you might decide that you wanted to live out there. I certainly would love to.[49]

He then suggests to Greg that a far better plan would be to find "a pleasant sunny place for Ada and Lorian" in Switzerland. It would cost a lot less than their total boat fares and expenses, and Greg could rest easy knowing that they were in good hands.

Of course, no letter from Ernest to Greg would be complete without an in-depth analysis of expenses, real and imagined. Greg had asked him for $2,500, and his father was going to give him that, but he didn't think it would be enough.

You cannot possibly make your trip on the budget you sent.
Truly Gig, I've figured it out . . .

Where your budget goes off is in items like rental car return Venice Paris. It would more likely be three times your figure. Also France, at least Paris, is one of the most expensive places in the world now . . .

About dough. When you have a capital of 11 to 15 million, like Winston, then it is right to use your capital. When you have an income, secure, of $7,000, you should never touch capital. On that income in Tanganyika you are a rich man, truly. Hang on to your capital and you might see some place you would want to buy and live out there. That would be O.K. But spending capital on exploration is not O.K. Any way not O.K. to make a reconnaissance with child and nurse . . .

About dough again. I have $6,046.81 in the bank. $33,000 income tax paid this year. $11,000 to pay on January 15 and expect $16,000 in royalties in February, which I will draw on to pay income tax. This leaves say $11,000 in the bank to maneuver on until March First. . I owe $75,000, which I must pay next year. I pay $320 a month for Mary's mother and father in the nursing home, which adds up to $3,840 per year, plus extra expenses, and is a little more than half of my total income from all securities which I had originally intended to be a reserve fund for when I was sick. My basic income, if I were ill and could not work, is about the same as yours and Mouse's.[50]

And after saying all that, he reiterated that Greg would be getting the $2,500 no matter what happened, and that if he won the Nobel Prize, he'd send him $5,000.

The next day, perhaps worried that what he'd written in three pages wasn't enough to convince Greg to rethink his plans, he said:

Everything that I wrote in the letter about the problems the
trip to Africa presents are as true as I could make them. I
could make them a lot more spooky and tell you what a
truly miserable time you could have on a long trip with that
many people but there is no sense in piling it on. Reading
it over I know I have not over-emphasized the danger to
both Lorian and Ada. There are all sorts of things that there
are no serums against.[51]

My father wasn't spooked, and said that he was much more
worried about the psychological harm that could come to a three-
year-old being left for three or four months with someone other
than her parents. It "can go a long way towards making that child
think you don't love ~~him~~ her and can do that child permanent
harm."[52] Obviously Greg was thinking of his own childhood here,
and how he'd been neglected by both of his parents. He was determined, at least until he suffered another nervous breakdown,
to give his daughter the love that he felt he'd never had as a little
boy. He wasn't trying to lay any guilt trip on Ernest, but he was
unwavering in his commitment to bring both Lorian and Ada to
Africa, and he did bring them. There were no hard feelings; he
just didn't want the same mistake committed twice.

When Ernest won the Nobel Prize for Literature in 1954,
Greg sent him a congratulatory cable, and his father sent him the
$5,000 that he'd promised. Reservations were finally confirmed,
and in March of 1955 they were traveling through France, and
then Italy, where they stopped in Cortina to ski. By April they
were in Africa at Patrick's place, and Greg wrote to Ernest that the
weather wasn't the greatest. It was the rainy season and hunting
was difficult, if not impossible.

In his memoir he says that he "shot eighteen elephants in
one month," and that he worked as an apprentice professional

hunter for three years. What he doesn't mention is the coffee plantation that he bought near Arusha. He spent a good deal of money on it—anywhere from a third to a half of what he'd inherited from his mother ($50,000)—but as an investment, it didn't pan out. Like any farmer, he would have had to stay there and work the land, but his heart wasn't in it. His calling wasn't in coffee, and on October 25, 1955, he wrote to his father that he'd be going back to the States in December. There weren't any medical schools in Arusha, and he wanted to finish his studies at UCLA. He had the transatlantic tickets booked, but his family left without him on Lorian's birthday. The affair that he'd had with the daughter of a local plantation owner effectively put an end to his marriage, and Jane and Lorian went back to Arkansas. He followed her a few months later, depressed and drinking heavily, thinking that he could make amends. He wanted to see Lorian, too, but was arrested for disturbing the peace in Arkadelphia, the small town where his wife and daughter were staying with Jane's sister. By that time, Jane had long since decided that enough was enough.

By September of 1956, the Defense Department had been notified of his newly reacquired status as a single man, and drafted him. At that point Greg decided to pay homage to his older brother Jack, and opted for the 82nd Airborne. Not everyone got assigned to the paratroopers. It was an elite unit, and according to Ted Hager, the 82nd's regimental surgeon and a good friend, my father said that Ernest and J. Edgar Hoover himself had pulled strings to get him in. When you think about the massive intelligence file that Edgar's FBI had been keeping on my grandfather since the end of the Spanish Civil War, this is somewhat hard to believe. But who knows—maybe he was telling the truth. Greg's induction into the army was written up in newspapers all over the country. Below a photo of him, looking very pale and serious, *The Washington Post* included the following caption: "*Hello to Arms*—Trying on a helmet is Gregory Hemingway, 24, son of novelist Ernest Hemingway. Inducted Monday, he hopes to become a paratrooper."

As fate would have it, he was sworn in on the fifth anniversary of his mother's death, October 1, 1956. Stationed at Fort Bragg in North Carolina, his career in the armed forces was short-lived, and came to an abrupt end just a few days into basic training when his bipolar condition got him sent to the "goony roost," the psychiatric ward of the Fort's hospital. Greg claimed that he couldn't run, and that the stress of the marches had caused him to have "panic attacks." As Hager explained it, "The training was extremely rigorous. You had to be in shape to do the jumps, and running was a big part of it. Greg was then assigned to the 504th medical company where I worked, and he seemed like a nice guy. I was hoping that he could stay with us, but the Army had already decided that he was on his way out."Greg was diagnosed as a schizoid-paranoiac, which wasn't correct considering that he was manic-depressive. He didn't tell his father, and once he was back in Miami waiting for his discharge papers, he got a job loading and unloading trucks. He wrote to Ernest that as soon as the papers arrived, he was going to apply for another passport. He wanted to return to Arusha to sell the plantation, and then afterwards, he planned to enroll in a summer course at Harvard, a move that he thought would help him get into medical school. As usual his father helped him out with his business problems, paying for his trip and expenses. En route to Africa, he stopped in Munich for a few days to visit Captain Hager.

The plantation deal—25,000 pounds to be paid off over three years—seemed secure enough. He'd hired one of the best legal firms in Nairobi to handle the transaction, and when it was signed, he decided to celebrate by inviting Ted Hager down from Munich for a safari. Hager was someone my father admired enormously. Their relationship would last for many years, and when Greg had to choose a hospital for his residency, he picked Mass General in Boston to be closer to his friend. Along with Robert Kyle (another fellow doctor whom he'd met at medical school), there was probably no one else in the world that he got along better with than Ted.

Ted Hager came down in May, and my father took him out to hunt for lions and water buffalo. But after he left, Greg shifted into another manic phase and wrote his friend a suicide note. "By the time you receive this I will probably be dead," it said. He sent it on a postcard. When he wasn't threatening to kill himself, he spent his time carousing in bars in Arusha and Nairobi before returning to the States, and then back again to Africa, and then finally to Miami, where he crashed. It was there that his manic traveling came to an end and Ernest had him hospitalized. He'd gone through all the money that he'd received as a down payment on the sale of his plantation, and would cost his father three times as much in medical bills.

At the end of August 1957, exactly three years before my birth, he wrote a short letter to Ernest, apologizing for the trouble he'd caused.

> I'm sorry that I got into this shape, but I will be out of here soon. If my check from Uncle Karl comes soon, I will be able to pay the hospital, but if it doesn't I will have to ask you to help me out until it does. Thanks for your advice in Key West. I should have taken it.
>
> Best love always,
>
> Gig[53]

Ernest did everything he could to help his son, as he always did for as long as anything still mattered to him emotionally. Toward the end of his life, when his own depression got the better of him and he would rage against Greg, the IRS, and anyone else who displeased him, Ernest would write a will that would leave his three sons virtually disinherited. But that was an expression of his illness, not of the man my father wanted so much to love.

While still relatively sane, Ernest took a keen interest in my father's cure, and wrote back to him on August 24, 1957:

Dear Gig:

Thanks very much for your two letters. I've talked to Dr. Jarrett and to Dr. Anderson and arranged to handle the hospital bills and the cost of your treatments as you asked in your letter of August 20, so do not worry about that.

I agree with you that talking with psychiatrists would never clear up your problems. You have certainly done plenty of that. But I agree with them that treatments such as Patrick had might very well clear up that anxiety state that made you keep moving from place to place and finally made you make those suicide statements and write notes such as you sent to Dr. Hager in Germany.

Even though you feel better now, the doctors have convinced me that it would be wise to take the same treatments Patrick had, and which did him so much good, so that you would not have a recurrence of that suicidal feeling and get rid of your anxiety state. They say that treatment cannot possibly do your brain any harm and they have made a most careful check physically.

It would be wonderful if it clears up everything as it did with Patrick. I only wish Dr. Hager had written me about the shape you were in and the reasons for your medical discharge at the time instead of waiting until you had sent him that postal card.

We want to do everything that can be done to make you well, Gig, and there is no use after a period of observation and good physical checking in putting off treatments that have a chance to make a healthy and happy life. I would have been delighted to send you back to Africa, but the way things were going it would not have been right for you to have been so far away with no one to look after you if you cracked up.

Now you can relax and not worry and know everything is being done so that you can go back to Africa in good physical and mental shape.

Do you have a good radio? If not, ask the hospital to rent you one. I will pick up the bill with the regular bill. The same holds true for magazines and books. If they let you have spending money during the treatment, let me know if you get short so I can send you some.

Not much news here. Trying to work under plenty of difficulties but know you will not worry about yours and take it as easy as you can and know that for once we are getting something constructive accomplished on these worries that have bothered you for so long. Then afterwards you can go ahead and work hard at something and be free of worry and be the old Giggy that we all love and are proud of.

Best love. Mary and all here send their love. Gregorio and Rene ask especially to be remembered to you. Your many friends here ask about you all the time and I always tell them you are fine—and I know you will be.

Much love,

Papa[54]

My father stayed in the clinic until the middle of October, when he was finally discharged. Ernest came up to Miami to meet him, and the two of them then drove down to Key West together. The plane to Cuba left from the island, but he also wanted to check on the old house. As far as I know it was the last time that Greg ever saw his father alive.

The electroshock therapy couldn't have helped much. On December 2, 1957, he was readmitted to the Miami Medical Center for another round of treatments, and remained hospitalized until the end of January. At this point Ernest was probably reaching his wit's end, having spent thousands of dollars on his son's medical bills and wondering when, if ever, Greg was going to come to his senses and stop spending money as soon as he got it. Speaking to one of Greg's doctors (or perhaps his own legal advisor), Ernest must have been told that he had to get serious about his son's finances. If left to his own devices, and if given enough fuel, Greg would burn up whatever liquidity he had. It was time to get proof that Greg didn't have the slightest idea of how ruinous his actions were, because only then could his income be put into a conservatorship.

I can only imagine how my father must have felt when he opened the letter Ernest sent him on January 20, 1958:

Gregory Hemingway
Miami Medical Center
1861 N.W. South River Drive
Miami, 32, Florida

Dear Gregory:

On receipt of this letter I must ask you to furnish me
A: with a complete list of your assets, your sources of

income, Piggott Land Company, Trust Company etc., and all of your present holdings in the U.S. and in Africa;

B: Please furnish me with the amounts of money paid you in 1957 from any source as income or as cash or loans or for the cashing of assets, and the amounts due to you in 1958 and the dates on which they should be paid;

C: Please furnish me proof that your income tax payments have been paid in 1957 and give me the name of the person paying this tax for you if it was paid by an agent;

D: Inform me what financial settlement was made with your wife at the time of your divorce and [sic] you are still paying her money for support of your child or for any other reason, and if so in what amounts, also what payments were made in 1957.

These requests are made in an attempt to determine your competence to handle your money. Any refusal to comply with the requests will be noted.

In March I loaned you money to return to Africa and to pay for an attorney to attempt to retrieve money you had invested in Tanganyika. You recovered a sizeable amount of money but made no repayment. You made between March and September one trip to Africa, another to the U.S., a second trip to Africa and another to the U.S. and had a return ticket to Africa via Pan American when—after repeated threats to kill yourself—you entered the Miami Medical Center on August 13, 1957, for diagnosis followed by electric-shock treatments for schyzophrenia. Your hospital bills totaled $1,750 which I paid. Copies of these itemized bills are at your disposal.

In October you left the hospital and accompanied me to Key West and said you were coming to Cuba. You cashed your Pan American Airways ticket for some $600 and in

Key West received some $4,500 from the Piggott Land Company. This check had been following you around in your travels.

You sent me a check for $1,000 which you said covered all your medical expenses. In reality it did not cover the sums you had borrowed to go to Africa to attempt to recover something on your investments there.

On December 2, 1957, you re-entered the Miami Medical Center, again under the diagnosis of relapsed schyzophrenia for additional electric-shock treatments and have been there at $150 per week until this date. I have been paying your bills.

You are now inviting friends to go on a safari to Angola this summer, telling them you have plenty of money to advance their expenses, etc.

Since you went through a large sum of capital which you recovered through my financing your trip to Africa and legal expenses in 1957, and received the sums I have mentioned in October of that same year and squandered money on purposeless trips, you will see the necessity of establishing your competence to administer your money in view of your schyzophrenia as established in September and again in December, as well as by your army discharge, which I have been informed was for schizoid paranoia. You now propose to attempt to re-enter medical school at Washington University.

So will you, as soon as possible, now that you have had several weeks' rest from your last treatments so that your memory is better, please give me this necessary information. If you cannot recall or ascertain these facts, you are certainly not in condition to enter Medical school nor to administer your money or property.

Your last Income Tax payment was due January 15, 1958. Since you have been squandering capital for a long time you may not have any tax liability. In any event your losses or gains should be properly computed and declared. April 15, 1958 is your deadline for final payment of 1957 Income Tax.

Please acknowledge receipt of this letter promptly.

I hope you are feeling much better. Dr. Anderson says you are doing very well but had requested additional treatments.

Excuse the necessary formality of this letter, but this is not a matter to be settled by talk, conversation, argument or pretext. It is necessary for you to give proof now that you know what state your affairs are in and to organize a presentation of this which is clear. I hope you will be able to do it, and that I will hear from you promptly.[55]

Greg never did write the letter that Ernest wanted. He knew that his father's tone was serious, and that he couldn't push him too far, but wasn't about to meet his demands—at least not entirely. He still had his pride, and instead of mechanically listing all his sources of income and property, he met his father's challenge and raised the ante, suggesting that he be given permission to manage the Key West house. The people who were living there were six months behind in their rent and Greg had a solution.

...I told them that if they didn't pay the $450, which will be one half the amount due them, they will have to move out. I also told them I had talked the matter over with you, Papa, and that you said that any decision I reached was O.K. with you. I know that we didn't discuss this particular problem when I called you on Sunday, Jan. 26, and you can of course veto my decision if you want to with a short note to the Nobles, but I hope you will back me up and let me manage this property because I am on the spot and therefore in the best position to do so. After I enter school on Feb. 3, I will come down to Key West at least once a month to look the place over and actually see that everything is running smoothly.[56]

Ernest wrote back to him that he didn't know that the tenants were so far back on their rent and that, yes, he would back Greg on this one. He was "delighted" that his son was taking an interest in the property, and hopefully now it wouldn't be just him putting money into it and getting nothing in return.

Greg had written to Ernest that the $1,050 he had in the bank would probably last him to the end of the school year, and his father agreed. He also repeated that he still wanted that statement on his finances, just in case the money Greg was expecting from Africa in March didn't turn up. Ernest wrote:

Times are really rough now and going to be much rougher. That is another reason I appreciate so much your wanting to help put the Key West property on a sound basis.

You sounded on the phone and in this last letter as though you were in pretty good touch with reality now, and reality from now on is a plenty tough horse to buck out. Everybody is going to have to know what they use for money, where it comes from and how to take care of it. Blowing it, throwing it away, or mis-using it is going to be just like throwing away water or wasting and spoiling supplies or ammunition in a besieged city.

Have Dr. Anderson paid up now through Jan 16 of this year. Will have the hospital paid when they send the final bill. None of these expenses can be deducted since you are not a dependent, so they come out of the small amount of money the Govt. allows me to keep. So it is fine to see that you are getting solid now and the important thing is for you not to blow it or get delusions of grandeur about it because money is terribly hard to get now and going to be harder.

When I have to worry about you I can't write. It knocks everything out of my head and this is the time I have to work or else. So will take a holiday on worrying now and knock off this letter and get back to work. Have been lashing myself to work for so long under difficulties, bad financial problems, no chance to get out on the boat for nearly two months with this godawful weather, too cold to swim in the pool, that am stale as a goat.

All your friends here and Bum and George send their best.

Love, Papa[57]

When he got out of the hospital, his friend Robert Kyle asked him to move in with him. Greg said that he didn't have any money, even though he wrote back to his father that he had $1,050 in the bank. Kyle told him that rent wasn't a problem; it was paid up through the end of the term, so they could worry about money then. Greg had by that time enrolled at the University of Miami and was taking the premed classes that he'd need to finish his degree and apply to med school.

By February 7, Ernest was again worried about his son's grip on reality. Greg had sent him what he claimed was the refund check for a Pan American flight to New York City that he'd never taken. He'd endorsed it over to Ernest, saying that it would go toward paying off the money Greg owed him. Ernest tried to cash

it, but discovered that it was not a check at all, but merely a receipt for a check that had probably already been cashed. Ernest
wrote to Greg:

> Will you please check on this. I could find out from Pan
> American whether the check had been cashed but did not
> want to embarrass you . . . The trip from Miami to NY was
> one I believe you made in August when you were to go up
> to Miami and see the Dr. but returned to K.W (Key West)
> and reported you hadn't been able to locate his office. You
> may not remember it or it may have been reported to me
> inaccurately. If you did not cash the check which was de-
> tached, presumably, from the Computation of Refund, it
> would be wise to find out who did. But first you should be
> absolutely sure you did not cash it.
>
> Please let me know about this and how things are at
> the University. Am waiting for the other letter. This makes
> it even more important.
>
> Best Always,
>
> Papa[58]

Greg never got back to him on that. Instead, they talked about
my dad's other financial worries in a phone conversation on
March 4 1958. Greg was having problems with his ex-wife, Jane,
and Ernest pointed out to him that signing over his trust fund
checks was probably illegal. For Ernest everything had to do with
taxes, and the more you could avoid paying by not making mistakes and getting fined for it, the better it was. Greg certainly resented the constant financial badgering from his father and
probably thought that Ernest was paranoid about the IRS. But
what he didn't know was that Ernest was getting a bum deal from

his lawyer, Alfred Rice. While his father was making a lot of money, he was also paying a lot of it to the government—much more than what he really should have owed.

It was a period when many of Ernest's problems were coming to a head. He had two and a half more years to live, and pressure was a constant. The pressure from his fame that had increased exponentially since winning the Nobel Prize. The pressure from his failing health, the hypertension, the long-term effects of the two airplane crashes that nearly killed him in Africa, his drinking, and finally, his inability to write the way he wanted to. The constant stress was changing him, emptying him of what creativity he still had, and many of the works that would be published posthumously were put aside at this time, with letters to his publisher saying that he just didn't have the strength to finish them.

Of course, in addition to his own problems, he had to help out his sons. Jack had had a crisis of his own, threatening to kill himself because he couldn't find a job out of the army. He was brought to Havana where Ernest found him a position as an insurance broker and where he could keep a closer eye on his eldest son.

Greg was always doing something to anger his father, and on May 1 1958, Ernest wrote a lengthy letter to Greg, detailing why his lack of confidence in Greg's business judgement was "as much a matter of the present as of the past." He complained that Greg had not been keeping up with the Key West properties as he had promised, and that he'd had to take matters into his own hands, renting one of the empty apartments. Ernest also complained about the African deal, which seemed to be going nowhere, and said that Greg couldn't expect much, not being there on the spot. Ernest wanted to know what was happening and thought, rightly enough, that his son was getting screwed. The plantation had been on the market for over a year after the initial deal fell through, but the man who was running it and in charge of finding a buyer was in no hurry. He was stealing money from Greg, and so long as there was no real pressure on him to sell, he couldn't be bothered. Finally, Ernest wondered why he was even writing such a long letter. What was the use?

> . . . Why in hell should I trust your ability to handle money? Not anymore, but any time ever since you ever had any money to handle.
>
> You're probably handling it OK now because you have very little, and so have to. Maybe you can learn that way to handle a larger sum. It certainly would be fine. But it will never happen in this world unless you apply yourself with diligence to salvaging the money that is due to you in Africa . . . Don't worry about having to write a letter with your bad wrist [Greg had broken it] now as you have nothing pending now except to keep me informed about your Africa business when you hear. You don't have to do that if it annoys you, but as long as you want to borrow money, it's better to keep in touch with your creditors. Just let me know about the wrist when you give me the gen on Africa . . . Been working very hard every day including Sundays. Gregorio was very sick for nearly three months . . . Bum [Jack] has been doing better this year. Started to get hot here.
>
> Love,
>
> Papa[59]

That summer Greg got a job as a pool lifeguard at the Clevelander Hotel on South Beach. His friend Robert Kyle was managing the pool, and the two of them lived for free in the small apartment atop the hotel. Greg wrote to his father in July that he'd been accepted to medical school at the University of Miami and that he didn't "need a Papa anymore." He meant no offense in saying this, he explained; it was just that he wanted to put things on a different footing. He was a man now and hoped to be treated as such.

The only problem was, he hadn't actually been accepted to medical school. He still had a number of premed credits to finish, and wouldn't be ready until the fall of 1959. He'd lied to Ernest, and then continued the lie by telling his father not to worry about him, because if it was too stressful he could always drop out and do something else. Finally, in October, he finished off the fabrication, saying that he'd decided not to go, that the stress was, in fact, too much, and that he was going to pursue a degree in zoology instead.

The last letter that still exists from Ernest to Greg is dated September 26, 1958. Ernest continued to write him after this date, but if copies of the letters were made, they were probably ordered destroyed by Mary, or forgotten in some dusty trunk in the basement of the Finca Vigía. The content of these letters couldn't have been very pleasant. While my father was living with Robert Kyle, before he got married to my mother, letters would arrive from Havana and would often remain on the dining-room table for weeks at a time before my father bothered opening them, if he ever did. Instead of throwing them out with the other piles of my father's newspapers and trash, Kyle kept many of the often violently polemic missives. When Greg, for instance, tried to calm his father down and keep him from worrying about the stress and what effect going to med school might have on him, Ernest shot back, "You don't need to become a doctor, you can live off my money!" Perhaps there were better ways to express disbelief in his son's abilities, but I don't think that Ernest used them. Not in the last two years of his life.

My father pushed ahead with his studies, and in between one manic phase and another, he hooked up with my mother, Alice

Thomas. It was Robert Kyle who introduced them. She was study-ing biochemistry and needed a microscope, and Kyle said that she could come over to their place and use the one they had.

Initially, my mother was as shy and socially impeded as my father could be debonair and engaging—and yet they hit it off. What began as nothing more than study sessions—where for months Greg would always accompany Alice back to her house afterwards—shifted into high gear the night my mother decided to sleep over instead of going home. Perhaps believing, as Ernest did, that if you loved a woman, then you should marry her, the two of them tied the knot three days later.

But being married never stopped my father from doing the things that he really enjoyed, and a week after taking his second set of vows to "love and to cherish until death do you part," he left his newly acquired bride in Miami to fly to Angola with Kyle and another med student friend, Gene Shoenfeld. The three of them were going to make a film on killing elephants, a spoof that in my father's eyes would deflate the importance of the "Great White Hunter." It would be a documentary that countered the Heming-way myth, directed by the black sheep of the family.

To save money, they traveled light. They brought a camera and some film and two rifles, .375 HH magnums, which they weren't exactly sure would bring down an elephant. They rented a Chevy pickup and slept in the open air without any tents, just mats on the ground. It was winter, and at almost 5,000 feet, it was freezing cold at night. When they weren't feeling the cold, they were notic-ing the lions that passed so close they could hear their breathing.

They were out there for about a month, and in the end my fa-ther had his film. Unfortunately, he lost it once he got back to Miami. Greg had the only copy, and his father complained about the enormous waste of money, certainly seeing it as yet another sign that Gigi would never amount to anything.

In spite of everything, however, Greg did get into medical school. He was accepted into the class of '59 at the University of Miami, and it looked as if this time, he would really go. He informed his father of the good news and made it as far as the dean's welcoming speech on the first day of classes when he dropped out. The stress was triggering another manic phase, and as he left the auditorium that day, he was convinced that he had to go to Paris and study at the Sorbonne. There, he thought, he'd find the peace of mind that he needed. The next day he and my mother packed their bags and left. Kyle tried to convince him to stay, but it was no use.

In France his mental condition took a turn for the worse, and after a month he was back in Florida without my mother, who he'd left in Paris. Kyle only found out that he'd returned when Greg showed up outside his window one morning, saying that he needed somewhere to crash. Kyle let him sleep on the couch, and Greg told him that he'd begun another series of electroshock treatments. My father was a great believer in ECT, the only cure that could pull him out of a deep depression, and said that after a cycle he felt so clean, so clear, that he was sure the treatments had raised his IQ level.

In the meantime, my mother was battling with her own tendencies, and sending him cables that weren't at all happy. She was saying that if he didn't come back and take her home, then she was going to jump into the Seine and kill herself. "Jump," my father would write back. He knew that she wouldn't do it, and in January, he went back to Paris to pick her up.

That year, 1960, he was accepted once again to the University of Miami medical school, and forwarded a copy of the acceptance letter to Ernest as proof that he wasn't making it up. His father accused him of squandering his money, and Greg countered that he had been living rather frugally, but that to finance his education he would need to sell the Key West house. Although the house wasn't sold, Greg somehow managed to get by on the little money that he still had.

In January of 1961, Ernest was admitted to the Mayo Clinic for electroshock treatments. Greg expressed his concern over Ernest's hospitalization in a letter: " . . . and I called the Mayo Clinic immediately, but Mary had left word that you were not to be disturbed by anyone, and as the doctor on duty took this quite literally, I was unable to reach you."[60] Ernest had tried to kill himself, the first of a number of attempts, and because Mary knew that Greg was someone who could send her husband into a fit of irrational rage, she kept them apart.

At this point, however, Ernest's problems had nothing to do with Greg, whose letters were calm, his handwriting steady. He was having a bit of difficulty with the second half of his first year, physiology and biochemistry were hard but Ernest had nothing to say during this period, when he was in and out of the clinic for treatments. There was one letter that Greg ended up writing (and sending) three times—the same exact letter with commentary on the Bay of Pigs invasion and a request for $500, with a postdated check to Ernest for the same amount. An IOU that Mary kept sending back—until the old man shot himself on the tiled porch of his Ketchum house, just short of the steps and the sloping hill where you could hear the river.

Chapter 11

THE FALLING OUT

Just as Greg's rapport with Ernest started to deteriorate in the 1950s, my relationship with my father took a turn for the worse thirty years later. After my last meeting with him by the river outside of Missoula, Greg went back to the stress-management clinic in Butte to continue his therapy, and my girlfriend and I were left without a set of wheels. When I tried to remind him that Ornella and I were sleeping in his Subaru because we didn't have an apartment anymore, and that he couldn't just leave us there, he said that he was sorry, but he needed the car. If we wanted to, we could camp outside the clinic, he told us, but whatever we decided, the car was staying with him.

As he left he forgot to take my set of keys, and after spending the day in a park near his old apartment, I decided to steal the car. We weren't getting anywhere in Missoula, and I wasn't about to repeat the mistake of counting on my father for help. He'd come off his manic high, but having lived with him once when he was on the right hand of God, I just didn't have the strength to do it again. I'd had enough of his pyrotechnical emotional output, of this synaptic roller coaster that linked him with his father, and at the same time, was simply part of his disease. I needed to get someplace where I could work, and where I wouldn't have to deal with this kind of stress. I was abandoning him when he probably needed me more than I needed him, but I couldn't help it.

I left Ornella in a twenty-four-hour Laundromat, telling her that I'd be back soon—which, when I think of all the things that could have gone wrong, was a fairly optimistic statement. I didn't know where anything was in Butte, had never been there aside from the Greyhound station, and had absolutely no idea of where the clinic was. But I really didn't have a choice, so I bought a ticket and got on the bus. Once in Butte, I asked for general directions and started walking. It must have been close to midnight, and the streets were deserted, with the exception of the odd pickup truck or cop car that passed by. I had to walk for about half an hour, past the old strip-mining pit that was now a tourist attraction, past rows of nondescript wooden houses, gas stations, and convenience stores, until finally I came to the clinic, exactly where they said it would be.

It was a one-storey redbrick building surrounded by a parking lot at the bottom of a slight incline. It didn't have a fence or a guard, and my father's red Subaru was set apart from the rest of the cars. I was afraid that someone would see me and call the police, so I tried to be quick without running. I must have looked ridiculous as I raced toward the car and the building where my father was sleeping, not two hundred feet away from the Subaru. I was as physically close as I'd ever be to my father before he died, but I wasn't going to see him. I was there to steal his car, and it never occurred to me how strange it was. I figured I was just doing what I had to do, tight-wired on feelings that my father had elicited, in a situation he had created. As usual he was pulling all the emotional strings, and if someone had told me even a week or two before that I'd end up running off with my dad's car, I would have laughed. But that was how it was with Greg. You never really knew how you'd react—only that you couldn't ignore him.

When I reached the car, I opened the door and put the keys in the ignition. The engine started right up, and I was soon back on the road north to Missoula. In the morning Ornella and I decided to head down to San Diego to stay with my friend, Henry Bisharat. I gave Henry's address to Abe, a real estate agent in Missoula who was a friend of my dad's. Abe had suggested that I do this because sooner or later Greg would want to know where I had taken his car.

After topping off the gas tank, I had less than ten dollars in my pocket. It was going to be a very lean dash down to the coast, I thought. We had a few sandwiches, some fruit, and a bottle of Coke to get us there, but Ornella couldn't have been happier. She liked to travel, and had I told her that we were heading for China that morning, her answer would have been, "Why not?"

Ornella wasn't a Hemingway, but she had more of my grandfather's spirit of adventure than I did. She'd spent most of her life, up until she was fifteen, in the same house, in the same town in Northern Ontario, and had counted the days until she was eighteen so she could get out on her own. In comparison, my childhood was fairly rootless, with my mother moving us around as soon as her voices told her that we had to go. I can remember ten different apartments before I was thirteen, as many schools, and all the friends I made that I'd never see again. We were a family of gypsies with my mother in control, and yet whenever we'd pack our bags, there was always this feeling in the back of my mind that I really didn't have to do this. That if I'd only stayed a little longer, everything would have worked out. My secret dream had always been to find a place where I could stay for the rest of my life and be happy, but I never did. I kept moving, like my father and my mother and Ernest, too.

By the time we got to Utah, I only had a quarter of a tank of gas left, so I called Henry to ask if he could wire us some cash. Instead he sent a Texaco credit card, which I figured would be just as good. He said that he was FedExing it, and that it'd be there the next morning. So we camped out at the airport in Salt Lake City to wait. The package arrived on time with the credit card and a little note from my friend. "Hope this helps," he wrote. But as we looked around for a Texaco service station, we finally came to the awful conclusion that there were none in the state of Utah. The Mormons, for some unfathomable reason, had excluded Texaco from their postmodern version of the Promised Land. They preferred Exxon and Shell to the "Man Who Wore the Star," and I was told that if that was the only card I had, then I'd better find some way of getting to Nevada if I wanted to use it.

This was definitely a problem. We were down to our last sandwich, and as I didn't want to wait around another day or two for my friend to send a different card, I got back on the interstate in the direction of Las Vegas. I figured that something would turn up, and it did. As we were cursing and joking about the Mormons and their teetotaler state, Ornella saw the hitchhiker at the side of the road.

He was a young man with longish blond hair, baggy pants, and a king-sized paper Coca-Cola cup that he used as a kind of purse. I pulled up in front of him and he opened the back door and got in.

"Thanks for stopping," he said.

"We're going to California," I told him. "How far you need to go?"

"California sounds fine."

"Good."

"My name's Terry," he told us. Looking at him through the rearview mirror, I thought that he couldn't have been more than twenty. He said that he'd been visiting some relatives in Salt Lake, and now he needed to get back home, which was outside of LA.

I had hitched rides several times while in Italy, but this was the first time that I had ever picked up anyone in the States, and I don't know that I would have done it had I had a full tank and some money. I was hoping he could contribute a little, and when I saw another gas station, I pulled in.

I told Terry about our situation, and that we needed to get out of the state to Nevada.

"Wish I could help you out," he said, "but I'm kinda broke myself."

"I see."

"But hey, don't you guys got anything you could barter? Like, I don't know, a watch or something?"

I couldn't think of anything, but Ornella started fishing through the glove compartment and pulled out the bowie knife that my dad had given me in Missoula. It was a hunting blade, beautifully proportioned and sharp enough to skin a deer. I'd had the last one he'd given me for ten years before losing it in Buffalo. I remember telling Greg how one of the transients at the shelter where I'd stayed had filched it (along with my sneakers) in the early morning before I got up, and the very next day Greg surprised me the bowie knife. He had a long history of giving me knives, and while I doubt that I ever would have used it hunting, it was a gift and reminded me of him. Nonetheless, as soon as I saw it, I knew I'd have to give it up.

"Try using this," I said, handing him the knife. Terry walked off toward the guy who ran the place, and I figured that he would get at least fifty for it. Brand new, it was worth double that, and it was only about a month old. With fifty dollars, or even forty, we could fill the tank and buy a few sandwiches and Cokes.

Terry talked to the man for a couple of minutes, and when he came back you could tell that it hadn't been much of a negotiation.

"Ten was all I could get out of him."

"That's it?"

"Take it or leave it," he said. And of course I took it. Losing the knife for so little teed me off, but what could I do? Getting over the state line was my first priority, and I'm sure that even my father would have approved. He liked to give gifts, but he didn't think much of personal possessions. If something was yours and it made you happy, fine, but if you could sell it and get yourself out of a jam, that was even better.

So with the extra gas, we made it to a Texaco station on the outskirts of Las Vegas, where I filled the tank, bought some food, and happily forged my friend's signature to pay for it all.

Terry didn't ask for anything, but I could tell that he was hungry, and insisted that he make himself a boloney sandwich. He had cuts on both of his hands that were open sores and wouldn't heal. He said that his eating had been irregular, but when he got to California, things were bound to improve.

"You should see a doctor once you're there," I told him, and he said that he would, just as soon as he got to where he was going.

Once out of Las Vegas, it didn't take us long to get to the state border and past that, into Death Valley, which in the middle of August looked more like Mars than anyplace on this planet. The air blowing in through my window was hot and dry like an oven, and in an effort to protect the skin on the left side of my face and neck from turning an even brighter red than it already was, I covered it with some of the cocoa butter from one of the jars my father had left in the car.

I was racing to get us to the sea—anyplace that would be cooler than where we were. The heat was unreal, and my only thought was that I couldn't stop until we got to the ocean. As the sun went down, we were on the outskirts of Los Angeles, and I asked Terry where he wanted to be dropped off. He had never told us exactly where his relatives lived, but he pointed to an off-ramp up ahead and said that we could leave him there, which is what I did. He got out of the car with his paper cup, hopped over a metal barrier, and shuffled down a grassy hill toward a traffic light in the middle of Burbank. He'd made it back to the city, and hopefully was telling us the truth when he said that he had a place to go.

It didn't take us long to get to Henry's place in San Diego. The traffic was light, and I knew the road. I was exhausted from the long drive and the heat, and must have seriously stunk after two days in the desert without a bath. In fact, one of the first things that Henry suggested I do was to take a shower. I was so tired that I was past the point of recognizing how much my stench must have overwhelmed my poor friend, and told him that I'd take a shower later.

"No, John, you need to take one *now*," he said, with great conviction. So, off I went to lather myself down with Ornella.

That first night, Henry and his two roommates, Phillip and Steve, let us sleep on the living-room floor. They had a big three-bedroom house on Mission Bay Drive, which belonged to Phillip's family. It was your typical large, suburban American dwelling from the 1960s. It had a front yard and a backyard, where we pitched our tent and slept for all the other nights that we stayed with Henry and his friends. It was a very hippie thing to do, and had it been 1968, something that might have even passed for normal. But instead it was 1985, and the people whose hospitality I often worried about abusing were hard-core Republicans. It was the height of the Reagan revolution, and while the president dreamed of Star Wars and his wife told the country to "Just say no," Henry and his friends were for me a further example that you should never judge a person solely on the basis of their political affiliation. People were usually more complicated and interesting than they appeared to be, and to this day what I remember most about San Diego is the generosity and goodwill of Henry and his roommates. We could use the bathroom and the kitchen, we were never charged anything, and they did just about everything they could to help me find work.

I met Henry during my first quarter at UCLA. We were in the same History 1A class taught by Sandra Dykstra in the days before she opened up her literary agency. Henry just introduced himself after one of Dykstra's lecture and from that time onwards we've been the best of friends, almost twenty-seven years now.

Steve worked for the city as a public relations consultant and was involved in, among other things, scouting out locations for the film *Top Gun*, which he told me was going to be a "huge success." He was also gay, and I think that the turbulent relationship I had with my father must have struck a chord with him. One day while we were in his car, he asked me if I loved my dad, "in spite of everything . . . because no matter what, he's still your dad, right?"

"Of course," I told him.

Greg would always be my father, for better or for worse. There was no real running from him. Wherever I'd go, a part of him would always be with me. I didn't know it then, or, if I did, I only half suspected it, but you can never cut yourself off entirely from who you are. Whether or not you understand the generations that went into making you, they can never be ignored.

What surprised me about Steve was the intensity of his question. No one had ever put it to me that way before. He really needed to hear that I hadn't given up on my father, that the bond was still there, and that eventually we'd be able to work things out. I don't think that he knew anything more about this than I did, or that he had any solutions to offer. He was just speaking from the heart, and I was impressed by his honesty.

It would take me years before I understood the importance of Steve's question—years before I could accept Greg as he was, and not as I might want him to be. San Diego was the beginning of that process. The point where I realized that I was on my own, and that maybe it was going to get a lot worse before it got better.

I would need time to grow, to flesh things out, but to do that I would need to survive. That meant finding a job. The first place I looked was the local paper. I didn't have any job skills apart from cutting wood and flipping burgers, so I figured that just about anything I could get would do. The first ad that caught my attention had something to do with sales, promising easy earnings and career advancement, with "no experience required." There was a number to call, so I dialed it. The lady who answered was the secretary for the California Integrated Retailers, and she said that there was an orientation on Thursday morning at eight if I wanted to come. I told her that I just might, and she gave me directions to the main office, located on the road next to the runway.

So I got up early on Thursday, told Ornella when I'd be back, more or less, and took my dad's car out to La Jolla and then due east for about three miles. The runway that ran parallel to the road belonged to the naval air base, and as I drove up to the building, two Tomcats were lifting off over the Pacific in the deafening roar of their afterburners.

It wasn't going to be much of a meeting, I thought, with these planes taking off every ten minutes, but inside it was absolutely quiet, and the blonde receptionist waved and pointed me in the direction of the conference room. The president, a tall, beefy guy named Perez, was there with a few of his close associates. They would later take our group—about twenty neophytes in all—around to show us the tools of the trade. Perez had Mediterranean features and straight black hair that was greased and brushed back from his forehead. He began his spiel by telling all of us that he knew what it was like to be hungry.

"And I don't mean just wondering where your next meal's gonna come from. No, I'm talking about a different kind of hunger. I'm talking about respect, and how when you don't have it and people won't give it to you because you don't look good or because you don't have any money in your pocket—that hurts!"

What this had to do with sales was beyond me, but I was curious. The company sold leather briefcases, and from what I'd heard it was pretty much door-to-door.

"Because that's exactly what we're offering you—*respect*," Perez continued. "A chance to own your own business and to build something new, becoming a part of an extensive franchising network that feels the same way you do about your career and your potential as a businessman in the larger statewide context."

Statewide? I thought.

"With offices in San Francisco, San Diego, and Los Angeles, we're a company that believes in growth and in the intrinsic worth of the individual. It's the man or the woman on his own who makes the difference here. Your talent and determination are the ingredients that we're looking for, and I just wanted to say, 'Welcome aboard.' "We all started clapping. I was curious to see what it would be like to actually sell one of the briefcases that were wrapped in plastic and sitting in cardboard boxes against the wall. As far as I knew, there was no one else in my family in door-to-door sales. Graduating from UCLA and spending a year in Italy hadn't exactly prepared me for this, but I was ready for a challenge. If I could make some money at it, I thought, why not?

Perez then introduced us to his staff of supervisors, and I and another woman my age, in her mid-twenties, were assigned to go with Rick, a quick-witted sales veteran who before coming to California Integrated Retails had spent three months under a bridge in between jobs.

We carried six of the leather bags out to Rick's car, which as a forecast of the day's sales was extremely optimistic. I sat in the front with our supervisor and Beth, my fellow trainee, sat in the back. Beth had just graduated from university that spring, and like me probably thought this was a way to make a quick buck without actually having to work that hard at it. She was on the tall side with straight brown hair and freckled skin that set off the string of white pearls around her neck. As we headed south on the freeway toward the Mission Bay area, Beth was enthusiastic. Rick was giving us a rundown, more or less, of what we'd be doing: essentially just watching Rick and learning everything we could from him about technique and pitch. It sounded easy enough, but when we got to where we were going and Rick started to strut his stuff, no one was biting. He certainly looked impressive as he'd approach total strangers and without a shade of doubt or hesitation ask them to shell out thirty bucks for a bag that wasn't worth more than five. He had the talk down pat and really seemed to enjoy what he was doing. He thrived on the contact, and while he wasn't obsessive in pursuing a mark, he didn't give up easily.

"Everyone loves a deal," he told us, "and you're the conduit. Remember: It's not an imposition—it's an opportunity."

But after an hour and a half Beth forsook a possible career in sales and said that she had to go. It wasn't what she had in mind, and she wasn't going to waste any more of her morning. Which was probably what I should have done too, but I liked Rick. I admired his courage and determination and was really hoping as the day progressed and we wandered from one part of San Diego to another that he'd make at least one sale. We sneaked into and were chased out of a legal office, tried our luck by the navy station and the zoo, and finished the day at a bar that overlooked the ocean, where Rick offered me a beer.

With the six leather bags safely locked away in the trunk of his car, Rick said that there were good days and bad, but if you were smart, you could learn from your mistakes. Of course, if you were on a roll and lucky, then everything went well and learning had little to do with it. That was the way it had been up until a month before, when Perez had chosen Rick's girlfriend to open up the San Francisco office, and she'd promptly ditched him.

"We were pretty much tied in terms of sales, so it could have just as easily been me going up there instead of her. Can't say that I hold it against her. I'm sure I would have done the same thing, but the boss said that I wasn't ready for that kind of responsibility and that I had to 'perfect my technique.' "

"And you can't go up there?"

"Got a job to do, here," he said, and ordered us both another beer. Getting dumped had hurt, but he'd accepted it, along with Perez's criticism, in order to further his career. Maybe that was all he had, but I didn't think so. He deserved better than this; anyone did. The whole thing was a sham, as much as the "Dianetics cure" had been for my father. A lot had changed since the 1950s, of course, but there was nothing new in sales.

When he took me back to my car I told him that I was sure he'd be the next one to get his own office, that Perez would finally come to his senses, but that I was going to look for something else. I needed work that paid, and thought that if after a year Rick was still nickel-and-diming it, then God only knew how long it would take me to get to his level. Back at the house I talked to Henry, and he suggested that I try the temp agency that he worked for. He lent me some of his clothes for the interview, and two days later I went to the Bolt offices with high hopes.

I had to fill out the usual application form, listing my education, job experience, address, and phone number. I gave it to the receptionist who then passed it on to my interviewer, Judy, a blonde woman in her mid-twenties who would also be my contact. She was the one who'd decide where I'd go from job to job. It took her about five seconds to realize that I wasn't qualified for anything besides manual labor, and she spent most of the remaining fifteen minutes that I was in her office asking me questions about Italy—where I'd been and what it was like.

She told me that the pay was minimum wage and that I had my first assignment the next morning. It was a job lifting furniture near the center of town, and I got there early in my dad's Subaru and waited. Another Bolt employee showed up, followed by the furniture truck. The driver was a short, stocky guy with an enormous beer belly, black jeans, and cowboy boots. He shook our hands, told us what we had to do, and opened the back doors of his truck. I was twenty-five years old then and in relatively good shape, but I hadn't done much heavy lifting, and by three o'clock in the afternoon when we finished, I was dead. I had the cowboy sign my assignment sheet and drove back home, thinking that if all the jobs were like this one, then I needed to find another line of work.

Luckily for me, there was heavy labor and not. Most of the assignments were just filling in, nothing backbreaking, just a bit of cleaning. Someone would give me a broom and tell me to go to it. On occasion, though, Judy would surprise me and send me out to a defense contractor or a research institute for a bit of variety. Around La Jolla and the university there were quite a few cancer institutes and I remember working in at least two of them. Actually, the first one wasn't really an institute (it was still a construction site), but at the second one, I did get to work in the "mouse factory."

What I didn't know at the time, and what I quickly found out, was that every cancer institute worthy of the name has its own live-animal division, or mouse factory. These were usually immense subterranean areas where at any given time a constant supply of white and oftentimes hairless mice was produced for the hundreds of experiments carried out in the laboratories upstairs.

The institute was in a beautiful location overlooking the Pacific, and after I parked my car I had to walk down a long, curved driveway that led to the basement. About halfway down, just before I could see the landing where the trucks would unload their live-animal crates, the stench hit me. A concentrated mix of mouse shit and piss that was unlike anything I'd ever encountered. I didn't know what to make of it, but kept telling myself that it had nothing to do with where I was going to work. Unfortunately, the closer I got to the building the thicker the stench became, until it covered everything, and I wondered how far I'd have to walk before I could breathe again.

"You from the temp agency?" said someone just as I saw a sign that read head office. I turned around and saw a tall man with a blond ponytail, checkered shirt, and jeans, looking at me.

"Bolt sent you?" he asked again.

"That's right," I said, and gave him my slip. He had a look at my name but didn't say anything. Usually at a new job, people would ask me if I was related, but he didn't. Probably figured that anyone who was coming to work here wouldn't be.

He said that I'd be working with the mice, and that if I was good and got past the trial period, they might move me up to the rabbits.

"And I'd still be working for Bolt?"

"No, you'd be working for us," he explained. I'd be given a serious job on the books, with the health care, vacation, and other benefits that came with it.

"Anything else besides the rabbits?" I asked.

"Primates, but you can forget about them." They'd had big trouble with animal-rights activists, he told me, and to access the chimps you needed special clearance. I asked him why, and he said that one of the workers had gotten too emotional about his charges, had started to disagree with what was being done at the institute, and had betrayed its trust in him.

"One night he let those fundamentalists in and they took off with our stock. Cleared out the whole ward, loaded 'em onto trucks, and then held a press conference in the desert. Mega-bad PR for the institute."

I'd heard about the activists and their crusade, and I was curious about the chimps, but figured that it was better to leave well enough alone. I needed to work and didn't want to give him any bad impressions.

I spent the first day in the rodent ward, counting the mice for their records, and then cleaning their cages in the afternoon before I went home. The mouse shit was in fiberglass silos, which were filled to the brim, sealed, and then shipped somewhere else for processing. The silos covered a quarter of the basement, and the stench that they generated was intense. At the end of the day my clothing was impregnated with the smell, and when I got back to the house Ornella wouldn't touch me until I took a shower.

For six of the seven days I was at the institute, that was all I did—count the mice and then clean their poop. But on the seventh day, the supervisor told me that I'd been assigned to section X. It was a smaller area upstairs next to the labs, away from the stench but still with the rodents. In the morning there wasn't much to do but sweep and look busy. I started to earn my pay after lunch with the cages. When an experiment was over and the mice or rats, hairless or normal-looking, were full of cancer, the technicians put them outside their lab doors so I could pick them up. It was something that happened every day, and the quantity of live animals that were used in these experiments was impressive. I began to stack the cages at the far end of the hall, and was wondering if I'd have to take them down to the mouse factory when the supervisor came and said that it was time to clean up.

"And the animals?" I asked him.

"Grab one of those garbage bags," he told me, and I did.

"Good. Now dump all the critters in the bag. Stick this hose in, give it a twist, and turn the knob on. It's CO_2. I'll be back in a couple of minutes to have a look." He went out and I was left holding the sack of panicked rodents. The mice and the rats were bouncing off each other, scrambling to get to the top before they'd sink to the bottom of the heap. There was no escape, and when I switched on the CO_2 I saw them gasp for air, jump a bit more, and then go limp.

The supervisor returned and asked how it had gone.

"All done," I told him.

"How do you feel?" he asked. "Okay?"

"All right, I suppose."

"Tell me if you have any problems with this."

"About the bag?"

"Yeah."

"No problems," I said, which wasn't exactly true. I'd gassed them, but I hadn't thought it was right, and he must have picked up on this because they didn't have me back the next day. They were looking for someone who could finish the job without any qualms, someone who could stick the hose in on a regular basis, and I didn't pass the test.

The cherry on the day's cake was the letter from my dad that I found when I got back to the house. He'd discovered my hiding place and was not in a good mood:

Dear John,

If you return my car to me within the next two weeks, I will not notify the Californian authorities that it is stolen!

I am in Missoula. Do you understand—it is simple! Return to Missoula with my car. I need it in my life. Go to Abe's—he will get in touch with me.

Dad[61]

Reading the letter, I knew that if I didn't get in touch with him, he would probably follow through on his threat and denounce me to the local cops. But just as he needed the Subaru in his life, so did I. Work in San Diego was hard to come by using the bus, and under no circumstances could I afford to give up the car.

I wanted to stay in California, and Mission Bay was as good a place as any other. The idea that Greg wanted his car back and was demanding that I bring it to him was both frightening and infuriating. I didn't feel bad about taking his car at the time, I needed it, but I did feel bad about having to give it back. I tried to imagine driving all the way up there just to hand him the keys, and then returning to California by bus. And then what? How would I survive without a car of my own? Everyone I knew in San Diego had one, and we didn't even have the money to buy a twenty-year-old pickup, much less pay rent for a room or an apartment. I was making minimum wage, and thanks to Henry's generosity I was able to save it, but if we stayed in the city, eventually we'd have to find a place of our own.

Of course, solutions can always be found, and had I not been so freaked out about seeing Greg again, I might have stayed, even with all of the problems I faced. Two of Ornella's friends, for instance, had offered to let us live with them on their sailboat at the marina. It would have been doable, but Greg's letter had brought back all of the craziness in Missoula, and it had left its mark. The feeling of helplessness and, in general, of having been used and abused by my father, was something that I couldn't overcome. I didn't have to stay with him in Montana. He just wanted his car back. But part of me panicked; I felt that if I went back there, Greg would do what he'd done before. This wasn't necessarily true, since he was no longer in a manic phase, but I wasn't thinking straight.

I showed the letter to Henry and Ornella, and they suggested I give him a call. When I did so, the big surprise for me was that he wasn't angry at all. He still wanted his car back, of course, but when I told him that I was working various jobs and that I didn't have the money to drive it up there right then and would need some more time, he was accommodating enough.

He gave me another month and tried to put it all in perspective, saying that had it been him, he probably would have done the same thing. He told me he'd found out where I was through Abe, and in the end, I said that I would call him again before I returned to Montana. But I never did get in touch

After my conversation with Greg, I told Ornella that we had to leave, and while she didn't want to and would have much preferred to stay in San Diego, she agreed to follow me back to Italy. To make more money I found a second job delivering pizzas in the evenings, and by the end of September I had saved up about $800. It wasn't much, but it was enough to get us two seats on a cheap flight to Brussels.

In LA I left the Subaru at the airport, and mailed the parking ticket and the keys to my father in a letter where I said that I was sorry, but I couldn't stay. I repeated the excuses that I'd been telling myself for the last month—that without a car it was difficult to find work, and that I wasn't making enough for rent—but I never mentioned the real problem. In reality, I was fleeing from the pressure of being his son, of being Ernest's grandson, and of having to understand all their pain. It was an instinctual more than a conscious act on my part, an unexpressed imperative that screamed "Get out and save yourself." Something that I'm sure Greg would have done himself, had he ever had the chance.

Chapter 12

THE WILDERNESS

My father got the letter I sent him about a week after we landed in Europe, but because he hadn't yet finished his court-mandated period of clinical observation, another fourteen days passed before he could fly down to LA and pick up the car. At first, the people who ran the parking lot didn't think that the Subaru was his. He'd lost the ticket and had to wait for the airport police to do a background check on him before he could finally pay and leave with the car.

He drove back to Montana, but he didn't stay there long. His license to practice in the state had been revoked after his last breakdown, and he figured that if he couldn't work as an MD in Montana, then he'd try his luck in Florida. His two oldest friends were still there, Ted Hager in Key Largo and Robert Kyle in Miami, and after a quick call to Kyle, he got in his red Subaru and left. He traveled light. Apart from the few dirty shirts and pairs of pants that he owned, the only other things he took with him on his cross-country move were the boxes of letters, pictures, and newspapers that filled the backseat and trunk space of his car.

Hager went down to the Keys in the winter, and said that when my father visited him in January of 1986, the clutter in his Subaru was impressive but that Greg didn't seem to care. Over a barbecue and beers they talked about old times, and my father told him that he was staying in a garage apartment across the street from Kyle's house. Kyle was the director of the Pharmacology Clinical Unit at the University of Miami, and Greg came to depend on him for many things. He was my father's enabler during the late 1980s, getting him treatment or medication when he needed it (Wellbutrin or Ritalin), introducing him to potential girlfriends, or just being there when he needed someone to talk to.

Greg wanted to work with Robert Kyle at the university, and Kyle had promised him a job if he could pass the Florida boards. Greg started to study for the examination, but he never took the test. The fear that he might fail triggered another manic phase, and in the depression that followed he gave up the idea of ever working again as an MD. At the age of fifty-six, and after twenty-five years of thinking of himself as a doctor, he understood that this period of his life was over.

Retiring wouldn't be a problem, even if he wasn't in charge of his finances anymore. When I was with him in Missoula, Greg said that Valerie had pulled a fast one on him after his last nervous breakdown. She'd sealed up his income in a conservatorship with an accountant who took care of his day-to-day needs. As he described it, she'd gone to see him with the legal documents when he was still in a hospital in Montana, recovering from a series of electroshock treatments. He was groggy and said that he hadn't realized what he was doing when she had him sign the papers that legally deprived him of any control over his earnings for the next ten years. Valerie, of course, had to think of her kids, and may have remembered how Greg would sometimes delay alimony payments to my mother, or send her checks that bounced.

It was her one chance, in fact, to avoid all the hassles that Alice had experienced, and she took it. Knowing what Greg was capable of, I probably would have done the same thing in her position, but, just the same, he was my father, and I felt sorry that circumstances had driven him to this.

Not that he was living all that badly; far from it. With the money that he got from the accountant, he could go out to dinner or the movies when he wanted to, fly over to the Bahamas for a bit of fishing, or move, as he did when he left the Grove, into the trendy area of Key Biscayne. He had a small apartment in a high-rise with a great view of the ocean, not too far from a one-storey, ranch-style hotel called the Silver Sands. When my parents were still married, we often went there for weekends, but even afterwards when they were divorced and Greg wasn't living with us, I went there.

The first time I met my stepbrother Brendan was at the Sands. Greg had taken a room with Val and her two kids at the hotel, and had decided that Key Biscayne was as good a place as any to break the ice and fill me in on the composition of his newest family. He had weekend visiting rights, and as we were driving from my mother's duplex on Louise Street, he said that a lot of things had changed in the months that we'd been apart, and that he had a surprise for me out at the beach. What I remember of the meeting in the hotel room was Val with her hesitant grin, her son Brendan, who was taller than me, and the baby, Sean, sleeping in a crib that they'd set on one of the beds. These were my new brothers, Greg told me, and while I was sure that that couldn't be true if the lady who was smiling at me wasn't my mother, I kept my opinions to myself. I was only seven and adjusting to a new set of facts and didn't want to say anything that might get me in trouble

The details of my father's first encounter with Valerie were something that I wouldn't hear about until he described them in his memoir. They developed an interest for each other at my grandfather's funeral, and if I ever thought that this was a strange way to pick up a future wife, his meeting with the woman who would become his fourth wife was just as curious.

One tale has it that Greg ran into Ida Mae Galliher during the "Pamplona Party" in Coconut Grove. Greg was cross-dressing at the time, and looking for a toilet in the ladies room of the Taurus bar when he saw this tall, hefty-looking blonde who had followed him in. Another, perhaps less-romantic, version of their meeting, says that Greg (dressed as a man) needed to buy a trophy, and he met Ida while browsing in a store that sold commemorative cups. They exchanged pleasantries, she helped him choose the trophy he wanted, and he left. She then found out where he lived, and the rest is history. Greg was eccentric, but everyone knew that he was the son of Ernest Hemingway, and Ida had a nose for money. She started stalking him, going to the same bars he went to, and soon enough, they were an item.

They were married in 1992 in the garden of the Key West house that my father had grown up in. Many of their friends from the Grove were invited, and Greg looked trim and healthy standing next to his new bride, who was at least a foot taller than he was. His hair was cut short, and from the pictures you couldn't tell that he'd had a breast implant. (He had only paid for one, probably just to see what it was like, and then never bothered to remove it or have another one implanted to "even out" his chest.)

The implant was one of the first concrete steps he took toward becoming a woman. For years he'd fantasized about the operation, and had even applied in the 1970s to a few of the centers in the United States where it was possible to have the surgery, but had always been rejected. The specialists didn't see him as being a true transsexual; at most, he was viewed as just another sexually dysfunctional manic-depressive with a fetish problem. But my father wouldn't take no for an answer. It became an obsession, and when, in the late 1980s, the testing involved in the choice of suitable candidates became less stringent, and private centers were opened, Greg knew that his moment had arrived. As soon as he regained control over the money from his father's estate, he applied to a clinic in Colorado; this time he was accepted.

Ida, like Valerie before her, threatened to divorce Greg if he went through with the sex change. She probably thought that his cross-dressing was tolerable, within limits, but that becoming a woman was not what she had bargained for. He underwent a series of operations, from November of 1994 to the spring of 1995. At the time my brother Patrick was spending a year in Italy and living with Ornella and I in Milan. I hadn't spoken to my father since 1987, but Patrick had a good rapport with Greg, and was a regular visitor to his Coconut Grove house. He knew Ida well, and while he said that he didn't trust her and that she was just staying with Greg for the money, he usually had to go through her to get to our father.

We found out about the operation from Ida. She called my brother, and when he hung up he shouted to me from the other end of the hall. "He finally did it!"

"Did what?" I asked him.

"Went ahead with the operation," Patrick said.

"Who?"

"Who do you think?"

Living in Italy, I had absolutely no idea of what Greg was up to. Whatever news made its way over the Atlantic usually came from my brother, and Patrick had never mentioned that a sex change was in the works. It's possible that even he didn't know about it. From the way he was looking at me, I could tell that he was sincerely surprised.

About a month after the big announcement, Ida called again and asked for my brother. I told her that he wasn't in and she said,

"Okay, then I'll talk to you." She sounded as if she'd been drinking and her voice was slurred. She was upset about Greg's operation and was filing for divorce. "I want a real man!" she whined, and I told her that unfortunately there wasn't much I could do for her. I'd never met her before and felt embarrassed discussing my dad with her. What he'd done to himself was neither my fault, nor my problem, and if she'd been foolish enough to marry him, then she could deal with the consequences herself.

In Milan in the early 1990s, I had little patience for anyone who put up with my father's behavior. Since 1987 I hadn't asked him for a penny. Whatever I had in my bank account was what I'd earned. It usually wasn't much but it was easier for me to deal with my relative poverty than the quasi-opportunist relationship that Greg seemed to expect from those who were close to him. Many people were using him for his money, and with a little effort, I could have been one of them, but I felt that it wasn't the right thing to do. In retrospect, perhaps it was just arrogance on my part, and as his son I could have followed suit—but I wanted something more. I needed a father, not an ATM, but I didn't have the strength to deal with his problems. I knew how similar he was to Ernest, but I hadn't yet read their letters to each other, so I couldn't see how that strange, almost mercenary, quality of their relationship was being repeated. It was a bad period, and in many ways I was as unhappy as he was. I'd left the States with the idea of becoming a writer, but didn't know that nothing good would ever come of my work until I could make peace with Greg and forgive him. I was blaming him for just about everything that was wrong with my life, which was ridiculous, but more time would have to pass before I could understand this.

At the end of Pat's sabbatical in Milan, he went back to Canada and found out where Greg was hiding. He'd taken a room at the Thunderbird Hotel in Missoula, where he was adjusting to his newfound status as a woman. My brother drove down there with his girlfriend, Denise, to touch base and see how he was doing.

The hotel owner told him where he was, and when Patrick knocked on the door, a rather unconvincing female voice on the other side asked who it was. My brother told him, and this time Greg spoke with his male voice.

"Pat?"

"Open up," said my brother, and Greg let them in. He was wearing female clothes and a wig and carried on with the split personality of his voices, addressing Pat in a masculine way and his girlfriend as he imagined the female part of him—called "Gloria"—would speak. Greg needed advice from Pat's girlfriend on just about everything. My brother told me how strange it was to hear Greg as he chatted away with Denise in Gloria's voice, asking her how he should cross his legs or put on makeup, and then suddenly turn to Pat and say in his gruff, masculine tone that there were beers in the fridge if he wanted one.

In late September Greg went back to Miami before the cold set in. He didn't have any place to stay, but it wasn't long before he was sleeping at Ida's. His old Subaru, the one I'd taken to California, had broken down, and he was using public transport to get around. Out in the open he usually dressed as a man, but on occasion, when he felt like expressing himself, he'd hop on a bus in his Gloria mode.

The day he went ballistic on the cops, he was Gloria. He was on his way back from Miami Beach to the Grove, and after a day of drinking, he was feeling frisky. Coming into a manic phase, he was doing his best to annoy the other passengers in the rear where he was sitting. He was wearing a dress and wig and was insisting to anyone within earshot that he was a woman, as good as any other, custom-made and ready to prove it. The driver was keeping an eye on him, and when he thought that Greg had gone beyond the point of just being a pest, he told him to sit down or to get off the bus.

Immediately Greg forgot about the passengers and charged up to the front to convince the driver that he was who he said he was.

He tried to act sexy and feminine in front of the driver, and the driver repeated what he'd told him before about piping down or getting off, saying that if Greg didn't shut up, he'd call the police.

But my father, beyond the point of no return in his wig and high heels, pulled up his skirt to show the driver his new set of genitals.

At that point, the driver made good on his promise. He pulled the bus over to the side of the road, and a few minutes later the police arrived. The first one on the scene tried to see if my father would come along without making a fuss. He told Greg that it was time to go, and when my father insisted that he really was a woman, the cop decided to put an end to his exhibition.

He reached for Greg's arm. But my father wouldn't budge, kicking the officer as hard as he could in the groin. The officer doubled over in pain, and it took another three men to subdue and remove a very ferocious Gloria from the bus.

Greg was arrested and booked into the Miami-Dade County Jail, where he had time to cool off before he was released on bail. Hitting a cop was a felony, and his lawyer advised him to plead guilty. Not too long before he was due to appear in court, Patrick went down to Miami to visit him. Greg had invited him well before the incident and his subsequent arrest, saying that he was looking forward to spending some time together, and that he'd meet Pat at the airport when he arrived. Greg never showed up, and Pat, thinking that he'd either forgotten or that he was playing one of his jokes, went over to Ida's house and waited. Two days passed, and just when he was about to give up, the phone rang. Speaking quickly and in a hushed voice, Greg told Patrick that he should go to this old motel in Coral Gables the next day and bring him a shirt, some pants, and a pair of shoes.

My brother drove over there with a brown paper bag full of the things Greg had asked for, and parked on the other side of the street from the motel. When Greg finally came out of his room, Pat saw him walk around the block twice. Apparently he was afraid that the police might be following him, and wanted to make sure that he hadn't blown his cover. Patrick said that he was wearing a dress and wasn't exactly inconspicuous as he tottered along in his high heels.

With no cops in sight, Greg nonchalantly stopped in front of the passenger window of Pat's car. In the same hushed voice that he'd used over the phone, he said that he was in trouble because he hadn't appeared in front of a judge to discuss his wrestling match with the police, and that it was his intention to flee the state. He didn't want to go to jail, and was starting to panic. Of course, it was almost impossible that the judge, fully aware of Greg's mental state, would have put him behind bars. Like his colleague in Missoula, he would have either forced Greg to seek psychiatric help or ordered him to a stress-management clinic.

Putting myself in my brother's shoes, I don't know how I would have reacted. At the time Pat was a lot closer to Greg than I was, and had probably grown used to his bizarre streak. He certainly knew him better than I did, but it must have been strange just the same to see him that way. Unsettling, if only for a second, to look at this person with the lipstick and the wig, who was grinning and whispering to you through the window, and to think that he (or, rather, she) was your father, and a Hemingway to boot. It wasn't exactly the picture that most people had when they thought of the great writer. But then, the public image of Ernest had never been more than half the story; the other half was with his youngest son.

Chapter 13

RECONCILIATION

After Ida's separation from my father, he had everything to gain. For a man with a guaranteed income of over a $100,000 a year, finding a place to crash might not seem like a problem, but it was. He was a disaster on his own, and when she took him back in, he had a place to stay, and at the same time, by not immediately re-marrying her, he'd given Ida an incentive to behave herself. According to Florida law, Ida's disgust with Greg's sex change and her subsequent divorce had cut her out of the family estate, and only if he wrote her into a new will, or remarried her, could she hope to get anything when he died. Still, it wasn't just Greg who benefited. In the brief period when they were together and still divorced, my father was paying her bills and in general financing her rather expensive tastes in cars and clothing. She needed the cash flow that only he could provide, and he needed a caretaker, in much the same way that Ernest had needed Mary.

But Ida wanted guarantees. The danger was that he could leave her someday, and she'd be left with nothing. He'd already gone beyond his father's record of three divorces, and there was no telling who he might meet or take a liking to. For Ida, the stress must have been intolerable. She was taking care of him, but he didn't feel the need to legally clarify their relationship. She had no right to the estate, and were he to die or to leave, she'd have to find a job. She could forget about their summers at the ranch in Montana, or the ego trip of being the daughter-in-law of America's greatest writer. She could also forget about managing the enormous wealth from the latest family venture, Hemingway Ltd. Profits from the new line of Ernest Hemingway home furnishings were about to skyrocket, and she wanted to be there when it happened. The only thing, in fact, that stood between her and a life of luxury was Greg's good judgment, or what remained of it. To get what she wanted she had to convince him to sign on the dotted line; she had to persuade him that he couldn't survive without her, that fundamentally he was too weak to live on his own—and she succeeded. In the spring of 1997 they tied the knot for the second time in a small town in the state of Washington. My Uncle Jack had a hunting lodge in the area, and both he and his wife Angela were invited to the wedding as witnesses.

When my brother Pat heard the news and asked Greg why he'd gone through with it, Greg said that he couldn't live on his own. He needed someone, and Ida was the only person willing to stay with him.

At around the same time my father and Ida were exchanging vows, my son Michael was born. Ornella and I were living in Milan, and while I didn't know what Greg was doing or where he was, I felt that my father had the right to know that he finally had a grandson. I hadn't spoken to him at that point for about ten years, but I was calling everyone I knew to tell them the good news. It just seemed natural that I should also phone Greg. The only number I had was the one in Miami, but he was in Montana when I called, so I left a message, short and to the point. I told him that I was now a father, how much the baby weighed at birth, and that if he wanted to, he could get in touch. I figured the ball was in his court. I had made the first move, and now it was up to him. I expected that he would want to talk. While the circumstances certainly warranted a conversation, he didn't get back to me.

Greg held grudges, and while it wasn't easy to get on his bad side, once you did, it was difficult to get back in his good graces. But more than that, I think that he was just afraid of getting hurt. I didn't know it then, but the distance I'd kept between the two of us was as painful for him as it was for me. I blamed him for our falling out, but for my father, it wasn't that simple. He was constantly reliving the events that led to his mother's death and the subsequent cooling of his relationship with Ernest. This unfortunately had an effect on his relationship with me.

In an interview with Stephen Crisman from 1997, my father said that he didn't talk with Papa for the last ten years of his life. From his letters it's obvious that this wasn't true. There was never a period when they weren't communicating. The relationship changed after Pauline's death, but never to the point where they weren't speaking to each other. What Crisman's interview did show was the extent to which he was confusing our estrangement with the far more damaging one that he'd experienced with Ernest. The lines between what had taken place in the 1950s and what was happening between the two of us had become so blurred, he couldn't recall where one began and the other ended.

Months passed after my call, and then a year, and by December of 1998, I'd long since given up on the idea of hearing from my father. I'd written him off, figuring that whatever excuse I'd had to make amends had disappeared, and also because I had too many other things to worry about. Italy, on the whole, is not where a young writer should go if he wants to live cheaply. The food is excellent, and nowhere else in the world will you find as many artistic treasures, but the cost of everything from clothing to gaso-line tends to be quite high, and this is especially true in Milan.

At the time, Ornella, Michael, and I were living in a two-room apartment near Piazzale Loreto, *un buco* (a hole in the wall), as the Italians say. Like most apartments in the city, it was over-priced, but doable with the two of us working. Ornella was a nurse at a cardiology clinic and I taught English to businessmen; while we were far from rich, we had enough to go out every now and then with our friends or to get away for the weekend. The problems started when Michael was born in 1997, and Ornella was fired from her job. She had just started working there and her contract was still temporary. When she told them she was pregnant, they told her that she had three months' maternity pay coming to her and then she'd be on her own.

So, in addition to the usual expenses that come with a new-born, I had to cover the rent and the utilities and everything else in between. I took on as much work as I could find, but freelance teaching is a seasonal job, and there was always the problem of the summer months (when the lessons dried up) wiping out anything I'd saved during the school year. What I really needed to do was get into another line of work, something that paid more and was steady, but still left me with enough time to write. Translating seemed a good solution to my problems. There was a lot of work in the city, and all I needed was a PC and an Internet connection.

But before that could happen, I had a heart attack.

Up until then, with the exception of my cavity-ridden teeth and a few bouts with influenza, I'd always thought of myself as fairly healthy. I didn't smoke, wasn't a heavy drinker, and as an amateur cyclist, I'd completed races in the Alps that could cover over 200 kilometers. Heart disease was absolutely the last thing I thought I'd ever need to worry about. So on the morning of December 10, 1998, when it suddenly felt as if someone were standing on my chest, I was genuinely surprised. Just before the attack I'd argued with Ornella, and still upset, I'd sat down at the table for breakfast. In that period I was picking fights with many people, using whatever excuses I could to let off steam and vent my anger. Ornella, as usual, was being extremely patient, but that day I must have been especially creative in provoking her.

When the occlusion cut off one of my coronaries, it was unlike anything I'd ever felt before, and it wouldn't stop. Immediately I told Ornella that something was wrong, and that I couldn't shake the pressure, but before she had a chance to do anything I got up and walked outside to buy a paper. I should have been lying still on the ground, or in bed, but instead was convinced that if I could just get up, I could walk it off. Without a doubt I was doing the worst thing you could do, but part of me had panicked. It wasn't until I was clear on the other side of the piazza that I realized I had to go back.

I thought that if I took a shower, the pressure would subside. As soon as I walked in our front door I headed straight for the bathroom. I got undressed and stood under the hot water, but the feeling was the same. The weight that was sitting in the center of my chest wouldn't disappear. My head felt like it was going to explode, and I kept asking myself why I couldn't get it to stop. I was seriously afraid, and it was then that Ornella told me to lie down and I listened to her. She had already called a friend of ours who was a doctor, and an ambulance was on its way to take me to the hospital.

The pressure began to subside just before the ambulance came. Whatever it was that was gumming up the works had moved on, I figured, and when the paramedics asked me how I felt, I said, "Better." They weren't convinced, and had already decided I needed blood tests and would be coming with them. I was thirty-eight years old at the time, and heart attacks at that age are generally of the unforgiving sort. They had reason to be worried, and I was helped down the stairs by the three of them, with my wife and my eighteen-month-old son watching.

Riding in the back of an ambulance was yet another experience I thought I'd never have. To cut through the mid-morning traffic, the driver turned on the siren and the flashing lights, but once we were at the emergency room of Fatebenefratelli Hospital in the center of the city, everything slowed down. I was handed over to one of the nurses there and taken to another room where I waited. I don't know how long I was in there, but there were other people there who had heart problems, and each of us was lying on what seemed like a cross between a bed and a servo-powered dental chair. There were buttons that I could press to raise or lower my back, but I didn't touch anything. When my name was finally called, they took me across the hall to another room where they did an EKG and asked me a few questions. The doctors were friendly enough, saying that it wasn't every day they had an American in the emergency room, much less one with a famous last name. Was I any relation, they asked?

"His grandson," I told them.

"*Non ci credo* (I don't believe it)," said the taller one.

"*Giuro* (I swear)," I told him, as his colleague quickly plunged a needle into my right forearm for the blood sample.

"*Ma che onore!*" (What an honor!) said the taller one. "*Curiamo il nipote del grande Hemingway.*" (We're taking care of the grandson of the great Hemingway.) They were both fervent admirers of my grandfather's works, and just my being in the same room with them was an unexpected treat. I'd made their day, and while I was more curious to know what was going to happen to me, when I could go home, and how long the tests would take, they weren't at all worried. I had put them in a good mood, and they said that I would have to stay in the hospital at least until my blood had been analyzed.

That, as it turned out, took about four hours. While I waited, I was parked in another room, which wasn't as high-tech as the first one. With its wooden chairs and unadorned clock hanging over the entrance, it reminded me of a small Italian railway station. The hospital, in fact, was one of the oldest in the city, and while you had wards that were very modern, there were other areas, apparently forgotten, that hadn't changed since the Fascists were in power.

As I waited there, I was convinced that they'd let me go home. I felt better. The pain was gone, and rather than feeling concerned about my heart, I was worrying more about my lessons and hoping that Ornella had called everyone to tell them why I hadn't shown up that day. In my line of work, if I wasn't there, I didn't get paid. I didn't have a safety net, and everything depended on my ability to teach and to keep appointments.

I was also worried about the bill. Italy, like all other European countries, has a national health care system, but at the time I wasn't on it. I could have been, by virtue of the fact that I was married to an Italian citizen, but I'd just never gotten around to doing it years ago when I should have, and up until this point, I'd never been ill enough to need hospital care. So when a doctor finally showed up with the test results from my blood sample and told me that I wouldn't be going home, I felt weak. I told her that there must be some mistake; I was fine, and I had to teach the next day.

"I'm afraid we're going to have to keep you here, Mr. Hemingway. We're never completely sure until we get the tests back, but your enzyme levels leave little room for doubt."

Something had happened to my heart, and the doctor was walking me up to intensive care. Before we got there, she agreed to let me call Ornella. I didn't have a cell phone and hadn't heard anything from her all day. I wanted to find out what had happened with my lessons, and of course, to let her know that I wouldn't be there that night. I really didn't know how long I was going to be kept at the hospital. Hopefully I'd be released the following day, but I wasn't counting on it.

I found a pay phone and dialed our number and told Ornella that I wouldn't be coming home that night, because the tests showed that something had happened to my heart, although I was sure that I was okay and that if it were up to me I would have left hours ago. Hearing her voice I felt weak again and it was all that I could do to keep from crying when I told her how much I loved her and missed her.

In intensive care I was plastered with electrodes and had an IV stuck in my left arm. It was dark outside, and that night I wasn't given anything to eat. There were three other patients in the unit, and from where I was, I could see their beds but couldn't make out their faces. There were two nurses on duty, and a doctor who came in from time to time whenever he was needed. I think that I dozed off for a while, and when I woke up I was surprised to be in that room. It was as if the heart attack had never happened, and I'd opened my eyes to discover that I was in a dream filled with white beds and glowing green monitors. It all seemed so strange, and when I finally remembered what had happened and why I was there, my heart started to beat faster. I could feel it pumping, and then suddenly there was a *pinging* from the monitor as I went into fibrillation.

One of the nurses noticed immediately and called the doctor, who was out in the hall. He looked at the monitor and without his having to say a word, the nurses were already preparing the injections. The younger one grabbed a glass bottle and a syringe as the sensation was slipping away from my fingertips. I wanted to tell them that something was wrong, but my lips felt funny and I couldn't talk. The doctor said that they could try the smaller dose in the IV, and if that didn't work, cut out the middlemen and go directly to the source. Plan B was an enormous needle about five inches long that they would stick directly into my heart. I'd watched the other nurse prepare it, thinking that it was much too big and not what I wanted, but that there was nothing I could do. Everything happened so quickly, and if the extra dose that the doctor ordered into the IV hadn't taken effect, I would have passed out.

"*Ecco,*" I heard the younger nurse say, "*si è stabilito.*" (He's stabilized.) My heart had started to beat regularly again, and I could feel the blood flowing back into my arms and fingertips. The doctor said something else to the nurses and then left the room. The emergency had passed, and Plan B was tossed into the trash. They may have given me something to sleep, I don't remember, but I was finally able to put an end to the day when I'd joined the illustrious club of Hemingway cardiopaths.

The next afternoon, Ornella came in to visit me with Mikey in tow. It was great to see him walk in with his mother. He looked so confident and happy and reminded me that nothing lasted forever, and that eventually I'd be home again. Ornella said that I shouldn't worry about anything, and that she was even working on the hospital bill angle with the police. In fact, a few days later she asked Paolo, a photographer friend of ours, to come in and take a few pictures of me for my *permesso* (resident's permit), which had expired, and without which I couldn't get on the national health care system.

They kept me in intensive care for two days, and then a normal room for another four, before I was transferred to a clinic that specialized in cardiology. In my work as a teacher and translator, I'd met quite a few doctors, and they took care of me in the week and a half I was hospitalized—especially Enzo Silani. He was the MD who had acted as my guardian angel in the Milanese medical community, organizing my transfer to the Centro Cardiologico. This was the best clinic of its kind in Milan, and among other equipment, it had a machine that could get a visual of what was going on inside my heart. I spent another six days in that clinic, mostly killing time or reading. I had an Italian translation of Asimov's Foundation series that I managed to finish, a travel guide on Cuba, and a couple of novels. The doctors ran a zillion tests, and in the end, when they'd determined that the occlusion in one of my peripheral coronaries was minor, they let me go home.

After twelve days, I finally got to sleep in my own bed. I was very happy to be back with my family, and getting out of the hospital in time for Christmas was the best present that I could have hoped for. It took me about a month before I fully recovered, but the worst was behind me. I was on beta-blockers and aspirin, and another drug to lower my cholesterol level. I still had the massive bruise on the right side of my groin where they had inserted the probe to take a video of my heart, but I could walk, and after a couple of days I made it down to the newsstand in the piazza to get a paper.

We celebrated New Year's Eve at home with a bottle of *spumante* and a *panettone,* and I was convinced that 1999 would be a better year. It certainly could not be any worse than 1998 had been. But even more than that, I knew I'd scraped the bottom of the barrel; that physically and psychologically, I'd been as low as I could possibly go, and there was nowhere to go but up. In the first few days after the attack, I'd often thought of my father in a negative way, blaming him for everything that had gone wrong in my life—from the stress that I'd had to deal with, to the faulty genes of my clogged coronaries. However, the illness forced me to look at things with a new perspective. He was nowhere near as bad as I made him out to be. Everyone had their weaknesses, and if I could learn to live with my own physical limitations, then perhaps I could learn to live with his, too.

According to my brother Patrick, and as I'd learned when I was younger, our father preferred letters to phone calls. If you had anything serious to say, then it was better to write it down. Calls were immediate and at times useful, but nothing compared to a handwritten letter. When Greg was away at boarding school, he usually communicated with his parents by writing, and whenever he had a favor to ask of his father, more often than not he did so in a letter. Ernest wrote letters to just about everyone he knew. He used them as a way of warming up before his work or winding down when he'd finished. It was his preferred way of keeping in touch, giving insider information (the true "gen"), and in general letting his friends and family know that he was still alive and kicking.

Whenever my brother needed something from Greg, he knew how to approach him, and when I told Pat that I was worried about the coming summer months and making rent, he said that Greg had just received some money from the estate, and if I wrote him now, he'd probably still have some left over. He got his inheritance in sizeable chunks during the year, but tended to spend everything as soon as it arrived. You had to be quick, because from one week to the next he could go from $90,000 in the bank to nothing. How he got rid of all that money so fast had always amazed me. I was working my ass off to make $15,000 a year if I was lucky, and he could easily spend that amount in an afternoon's shopping spree on designer shoes and dresses.

I honestly had my doubts about a letter working after all this time, but then I thought, What have I got to lose? I'd either hear from him or I wouldn't, and when I sat down to write, I finally apologized for what had happened in Montana and for ripping off his car. I said that I had been under a lot of stress and had panicked, and that I needed his help. I told him about the heart attack and the week I'd spent in intensive care, and said (lying, of course) that I had some major medical bills to deal with. Ornella did manage to get me on the national health care plan. I asked him for

$5,000, and said that if he didn't want to get in touch with me again, I'd understand, but that at least I'd finally gotten around to writing a letter that should have been written years before.

To my great surprise, my brother was right. Letters were more effective than phone calls with our father. He wrote back saying that it was great to hear from me and repeated what he'd told me over the phone in San Diego, that as far as stealing the car went, he would have done the same thing in my shoes. He included a check for the five thousand, and said that if I ever needed anything else, or just wanted to chat, to give him a call.

His letter wasn't very long, just a couple of paragraphs, but I think I must have read it about ten times that day. The handwriting was the same, and the signature, too, though I noticed he no longer put the md after his name on the address. I had about five hours of teaching that afternoon in different parts of the city, and I carried the letter with me in my pocket, touching it from time to time to remind myself that I still had a father and that everything was okay.

When I got home after work, I decided to give him a call. Ida answered the phone, and when I told her who I was, she went running through the house to get Greg. It took him a while to get to the living room because he had bad hips and was using a walker to get around.

"John, is that you?" he asked, in a voice that had a higher pitch than I remembered. He also sounded older, but I couldn't tell if he was faking it or not. In truth, there was no real reason for me to think this wasn't the way he sounded. Everyone got older, and we hadn't spoken to each other for ten years.

I thanked him for the letter and the check, and he said that he was happy to help me out, and sorry to hear about my heart problems. He asked about Ornella, who he remembered quite well, and about Michael. He'd never seen a picture of his grandson, and I told him that I'd send him some photos if he liked.

"That would be swell," he said.

"And I'll make it a point to write more often," I told him. "No sense in waiting another ten years."

He laughed, and then surprised me by saying something that had nothing to do with the letters or Michael—that essentially we could never be as close as we were when I was a boy.

"That can't be repeated," he said, almost as if he was trying to end the conversation on a note of reality.

I said that that was a long time ago, and we could work on it, make it even better. But for Greg, that wasn't the problem. There were only a few chances for happiness in anyone's life, and you either took them or didn't. When they were gone, you couldn't bring them back or pretend that time hadn't passed. The relationship that we'd had, the days when he'd been my hero in the Jaguar, reminded him of his own father and of an innocence that had ended too soon.

But in spite of his initial pessimism, our rapport did improve. While nothing could be repeated, perhaps we were starting something new—or at least that's what I liked to think. We continued to write, and I included pictures of Michael in my letters. My son bore a striking resemblance to Greg, and it reminded me how looks oftentimes skipped a generation.

Sometimes Greg would call even when it was the middle of the night in Milan. In his late sixties by now, he wasn't very good at keeping track of the time difference between one continent and another, and I remember conversations at three in the morning when he'd be burning with energy and I was barely awake. If I called him, though, it was rare that he'd actually answer the phone. Ida was the one who usually picked up. She acted as a kind of filter for his calls, and at the time I thought that if I were ever to get on this woman's bad side, I wouldn't be hearing much more from my father. He'd taken her on as his caretaker, and that's exactly what she did, up to a certain point.

In the summer of 2000, I asked him for another loan, but my younger sister Vanessa was getting married then, and he said that he'd already spent everything from the last estate check on her wedding. He was terribly sorry, but he couldn't help me out. He told me that Ida was the banker in the family and that if it were up to him, he'd send me whatever I wanted tomorrow, but that his wife had put the brakes on his generosity and I'd have to wait. While part of me found it hard to believe that he could be so down in the dumps financially (was he or was he not the son of Ernest Hemingway?), there really wasn't much that I could do. I had thought of buying a used car, a Fiat or a cheap VW, but put it off and instead spent the summer translating a Web site to keep the bills at bay.

In the fall I told my brother Pat about Ida's interference, and he repeated what he'd told me before about catching Greg at the right time. If you weren't there when the estate checks came in, then you could forget about it. Our father gave new meaning to the word "speed" in consumer spending, and was probably telling me the truth when he said that he didn't have anything. You just had to keep trying until you got lucky. All of this might sound bizarre to many people outside our family, but that was the way you had to deal with Greg, on his terms. He expected the requests from us and I think he relished being able to act like a sugar-daddy from time to time, much in the same way that Ernest had with him in the 1940s and '50s.

Of course, there was no way of knowing how he'd feel about sending you a check even if he did have the funds. Just because you were his son wasn't a guarantee. It didn't hurt that you were related, but I never managed to escape that feeling of uncertainty when dealing with my father. I thought it a question of pure chance if he helped you out, of all the right elements falling into place, and then *Bingo!* Generosity appeared and I could pretend, once again, that I came from a "normal" family. And so, not really expecting anything, I wrote him another letter. I wanted to buy a new PC for my translating work, and this time, perhaps feeling bad about the summer, he gave me what I'd asked for and a little extra, along with a note thanking me for the latest photos I'd sent him of Michael.

After Christmas my cousin Hilary asked me to contribute a few pages to a book she was writing at the time on Ernest and Bimini, She'd already contacted my Uncle Patrick and Valerie and had even tried calling my father, but Greg was feeling depressed and said that he wasn't up to it. She didn't have a publisher yet, but didn't think there'd be any problem finding one, and told me that if all went well, the book would come out the following summer. There were no guidelines, other than it had to be about the island. I wrote about my weekends there as a child with my parents, and about Ernest. For me it was an exciting project, because apart from being given the opportunity to describe a place that I'd always loved and to have it published, I also thought that if I did it right, then people might remember a different Greg.

I finished it in about a week. It took me a couple of days to get the tone right in the beginning, but once I'd settled on a description of my parents, and flying over there, and the colors of the water that would change from a deep blue to a green to a transparent white over the sand, the rest of the story came easily enough. I wrote about the people, the bars, and the Red Lion restaurant where we used to eat. I wondered if anything had changed and if the fishing would still be the same as it had been when my father would pay for a day's charter on Captain Bob's wooden Bertram. In the 1960s there were literally no limits to what you could find in the Gulf Steam. The overfishing and the conservation groups that you hear about now didn't exist then, and I wrote about the picture of Greg standing on Weech's dock next to the marlin he'd taken in his hospital whites.

But I also wrote about my grandfather and his boxing:

Ernest certainly didn't need to box, but he liked the sport, and more importantly, I think, liked putting himself on the line. Primitive, brutal, and yet in its own way elegant, boxing was a test for him. It was another way for this writer who was never satisfied with what he achieved to push his limits. Up there in the ring everything is stripped down to the bare essentials. If you win it's because you're a better boxer, and if you lose, there are no excuses. A mirror of the kind of clarity that you find in his writing and that he must have found invigorating. Likewise, I think that the fishing that he did, more than influencing his writing, was something that he needed, a tonic that he couldn't live without. They were the moments of Zen-like acuity where the powerful strokes of soaring marlin renewed his faith in the things that for him counted.

The paragraph reflected what I thought, and what I continue to think to be the core of his greatness as a writer. My Bimini piece is essentially a tribute to my father, but when it came to Ernest, I had to give credit where credit was due. He may have had a troubled relationship with his son, but as an artist he was sublime, a genius whose work has more than withstood the test of time.

I e-mailed Hilary a copy of my piece and faxed a copy to my dad. Hilary wrote back to me the same day, saying that I had honored my dad and that it was fantastic writing. I also sent it out to some other relatives and friends, and everyone agreed that I'd done a great job, but I still hadn't heard anything from my father. I sent the fax again just to be sure, and double-checked the confirmation slip from the machine. Everything was as it should have been, and yet he still didn't call or write. After a week and a half I was beginning to think that maybe he didn't like it.

I told Hilary about the faxes and how I had yet to hear from him, and she decided to mail him a copy of my chapter. Another week passed and my cousin wrote back with some good news. Her letter with a copy of my chapter got through to Greg, and he liked it. Not only that, but the weekend that it arrived, Hilary was away and my father kept leaving messages on her answering machine. He wanted to tell her how much he appreciated her sending it, and even if at times it sounded as if he'd been drinking, the sincerity of what he was saying was undeniable. His excuse for filling up the memory card of her answering machine was that he had lost the envelope with her address and that he really preferred writing, but obviously couldn't, and so he was phoning to let her know how he felt. He had my number, I was sure of this, but that first weekend I don't think that he would have been able to talk to me.

The chapter, as my brother Pat would later say, had touched Greg's heart. I'd succeeded in giving him back, temporarily at least, some of the dignity that his manic condition, frail health, expulsion from his profession, and verbally abusive wife had taken away. I'd reminded him of a time when he was not the "freak" that he sometimes called himself. In my mind he would always be a doctor with a young son who adored him, and no one would ever be able to take that memory away. It was his for as long as he lived, and my chapter was proof of this, and proof that there were still people who remembered him the way he'd been.

Hilary said that I should call him, and she asked if I had his number. I told her that I did, and after a few days of trying, I finally got in touch with him on one of the rare occasions when Ida wasn't there to screen his calls.

He told me that my chapter on Bimini was one of the best things written by anyone in the family since his father, and that it was a shame that he hadn't been more supportive of my writing in the past. It was something that he wanted to make up to me if he could, and that what I needed in his opinion was time to get away on my own. Writing time where I wouldn't have to worry about the day-to-day distractions of paying bills and rent, and where I'd be inspired by the beauty of my new surroundings. He suggested that I go to South Africa and said that he'd be willing to foot the bill, whatever the cost. I don't know why he was so interested in South Africa, but the idea of my living there appealed to him immensely. He wanted me to write a book while I was down there, or something that I could get published. He felt this would jump-start my career.

There was only one string attached to his offer: I had to come up with a detailed plan for the trip.

"Even if it costs $100,000," he said, "I'm good for it, believe me, but I want a plan." And I told him that I'd think about it and get back to him in a few days.

I had to admit he sounded serious, and my mother's brother also thought that Greg wasn't bluffing. He hadn't spoken to Greg in years, but after calling him up he came away from their conversation convinced of two things: that Greg really wanted to help me, and that he had the money to do so.

But my initial objection was that I couldn't just leave my wife and son in Milan while I went down to South Africa to make believe that I was a "Hemingway writer." What would they live on while I was gone? And when I got back, what would we live on if what I wrote wasn't good enough to be published? After years of having to make do on next to nothing, there was an element of risk in my dad's offer that I didn't like. In retrospect, I could have just as easily taken Ornella and Michael with me on the trip, pumping up my expense account in ways that my father never would have noticed. Nor was it written that I had to go back to Milan and continue teaching English once I'd finished with

South Africa. My father was offering me something enormous here—the chance to explore a new culture and country, and something good would have come of it, had I been ready. But I was too worried about his reliability and couldn't see what this gift meant to him. I hadn't read the letters that he and his father had written to each other in the 1950s, and knew nothing about how Ernest had financed his trip to Africa.

For Greg, sending me down to Africa was a way of showing his affection, as it had been for his father, and seeing as how I wanted to write and he thought I had some talent, it would also be a way to stimulate my creativity, just as traveling had no doubt stimulated Ernest's creative vein. It was the natural thing to do, given his history with Ernest, and had I been a bit more trusting and willing to take a chance, I might have said yes. Instead, I called him back after a week and told him that I couldn't go. I appreciated the offer and said that if he wanted to, he could help me out with the bills while I continued my writing at home. Greg was gracious and quite understanding, but there was no mistaking the disappointment in his voice.

My efforts to come up with something else that he'd like, to justify his help and perhaps even his attention, were far from successful. Greg was never one to beat around the bush. If he thought that a story was subpar, or that it sucked, he said so. He might have had trouble coming to terms with his relationship with Ernest, or with his own sexuality, but he could be brutally honest about my work. With his father as a standard, anyone in the family who decided to write had a hard act to follow, putting it mildly, and I'm sure that Greg thought he was doing me a favor. He knew that, if anything, whatever I wrote would be judged just as harshly or even more so by others.

After the Bimini piece, I sent him a short story, and he told me that it wasn't very good. He said that it was rushed, trite, and stereotyped, and that he really couldn't understand what it was I was trying to say. But he also said that even his father had had his "off" days, and while that didn't happen very often, when Ernest wrote something bad, it was *really* bad.

"So there," he told me, "everyone can screw up. It's no crime. The important thing is not to kid yourself and to move on, and to write every day."

I didn't like what he had to say, but he was right. I was trying too hard, forcing something that had to come out on its own. I wrote a few other stories, but his initial enthusiasm faded quickly. With my father you had to strike while the iron was hot, or not at all.

He may have given up on me as a writer, or the son to whom he'd "passed on Papa's genes," but we continued to call each other, and I would send him pictures of Michael and short letters where I'd let him know what I was up to. It was a comfortable-enough relationship, except when it came to money. The South Africa trip was an exception to the rule. Usually he would promise a thousand or two thousand dollars when I'd ask, saying that he'd sent the check, and when the check wouldn't arrive, I'd call him again and ever so politely inquire if perhaps he hadn't remembered to post the letter, or suggest that maybe the address was wrong or that he'd forgotten to buy a stamp.

In the back of my mind I knew that it was a mistake to do this. I loved him, but I shouldn't have been depending on him, and not just because he wasn't reliable. What kind of relationship was it where I was always asking him for money? It was what he expected, but wasn't that in itself wrong, and exactly what I'd refused to do for the ten years when we weren't talking to each other? I still couldn't get used to it, and even if it had been the other way around in the 1950s (where he'd been on the receiving end with Ernest), that was hardly a justification. But then I'd think that if he could help my other brothers and sisters from time to time, then why shouldn't I give it a go? Plus, I couldn't really expect a change in our rapport if I didn't keep in touch with him, and with Greg it had to be on his terms, which usually translated into a never-ending game of emotional financial tag.

The last time I spoke to my father, he was in Montana. He had just finished rereading the Bimini chapter with my brother Pat, and was in a talkative mood. He'd had his bad hips replaced and had been off his medication since the middle of July and was well into a manic phase by the end of August. Greg was someone who liked his highs, and when my brother went there for a weekend with his girlfriend, things were definitely getting out of hand.

"I've been down here three days but I don't know how much longer I can take this," said Pat. We were on the phone even though it was two in the morning in Milan. The initial idea had been for all of them to go white-water rafting on the Snake River. It was the kind of trip that my dad was always planning, but instead of leaving, they sat around the ranch while the lava dome of Greg's volcanic temper grew.

"He wanted to read the story and I thought that it would be a good idea, that it might calm him down," said Pat. "And then we read it and I said, 'Hey, why don't we call John?' And he said, 'Sure, Pat, you do that while I grab some more beers.' So, now he's in the kitchen, and I don't have much time, but when he comes back, pretend like you just got on the phone, okay? He's flipping big-time, and I gotta get outta here before he does something dumb."

My brother had a great deal of experience dealing with our dad in his manic phases, much more than I did, and if he said that it was bad, then I could be sure that he was telling the truth. I'd seen him sixteen years ago in Missoula, and once was enough to know that here was a man who liked to provoke, and he could be extremely good at it when there was nothing to hold him back.

"Hey, John!" Greg said when Pat handed him the receiver.

"Dad."

"Listen up—we just finished reading your piece on Bimini, and it's great stuff, really good writing."

"Thanks."

"No, seriously, you really pulled the rabbit out of your hat with this one."

"Okay."

"No, not just 'okay,' I *mean* it."

"And I believe you."

"Well, maybe you don't, but it doesn't matter." And I could tell from the sound of his voice that he'd been drinking. It was the quick, slightly slurred combination of the booze and his manic energy that I heard.

"It's very good," he said.

"Thanks," I said again.

"But why did you have to write all those nice things about Papa?"

"Nice things?"

"I mean, all that stuff about the boxing, the sea, and the shit about pushing limits. Why did you have to say that?" And I was surprised that he should mention it.

"I had to write something," I told him.

"Well, you shouldn't have, 'cause he didn't deserve it."

While I knew that he was on a manic high, and that every-thing he said had to be taken with a grain of salt, I was still sur-prised by the intensity of his feelings. It seemed nothing had changed or been resolved from when his father died, and no one, not even his eldest son, could paint a pretty picture of Ernest and get away with it.

Chapter 14

END GAME

My father flew down to Miami at the beginning of September 2001, soon after my conversation with him. Ida wasn't very happy that he was leaving, thinking of his past spending sprees and the enormous credit card bills that he had run up, and before he left she told him that if he got arrested again and put in jail, then he could rot there for all she cared. The threat was very much in keeping with her style, and Greg didn't take her too seriously. My father was in a manic good mood and more than happy to get away from his alcoholic, money-grubbing wife. If she wanted to sit in Montana and wrap up the sale on their house, fine, she could stay there. He was going to Miami, and as soon as he was back in Florida he started to think about how he might survive on his own.

Less than a week after he arrived, the Twin Towers in New York City came tumbling down, and all commercial flights in the United States were grounded. Like most Americans, my father was shocked by the magnitude of the disaster, but in the frenzy of his manic high he was also thinking that the general fall in airline stocks on Wall Street could be played to his advantage. His plan was to invest everything he had in United and American Airlines stocks while they could be picked up for next to nothing, and then make a killing when the federal government inevitably came to the industry's rescue and bailed it out to the tune of billions of dollars. He had a few million to invest, and with the money that he'd make, he would set up individual trust funds for all of his eight children.

From his command center at the house in Coconut Grove, he made calls to his broker at Merrill Lynch and told him that he wanted to put everything he had into these stocks. The broker agreed that the two airlines involved in the hijackings would eventually rebound, and that banking on an upturn wasn't such a bad idea. It was the right time to take a chance, but my father's plan didn't last long. When Ida got wind of what her husband was doing, she immediately called the broker with orders to stop it. She also phoned their bank in Coconut Grove and put a freeze on their account so that Greg couldn't use any of the money or any of the credit cards that he had with him. The idea of having all their money disappearing into dirt-cheap airline stocks must have been a tremendous shock and a wake-up call for Ida. That was not at all how she wanted to have her eventual retirement funds spent, and she was forced to act quickly to nip this form of creative financing in the bud.

The result was that from one day to the next, Greg found himself penniless and reduced to begging in front of liquor stores for handouts. One store on the corner of Bird Road and University Boulevard was in an older building. It was typical of the hurricane-savvy construction of the early 1960s, with thick, concrete-block walls and relatively small windows. As a boy I had ridden by it many times on my way to and from our house on Mary Street. Everything around the store had changed, but the building was the same, and it was there that a friend of Greg's saw him with a plastic Coke cup, begging for money. He was dressed as a man, wearing a pair of tennis shorts, old sneakers, and a T-shirt. His friend asked him if he needed a place to crash. Greg, of course, had a place to stay—Ida's house—but he hadn't eaten anything that day and was hungry. It was also good just to be able to talk to a friend who would listen to him as he rambled on at manic speed.

For Greg, having his credit cards blocked and his account frozen was the last straw. Ida was dead meat as far as he was concerned. He knew that she was obsessed with money, and while he was philosophical about the power of love, any woman who could do this to him wasn't exactly a devoted wife. He would have to cut her out of his life, and once he'd made up his mind there could be no turning back. She was playing hardball, and he couldn't leave her and then beg her forgiveness when he discovered that solitude wasn't his cup of tea. But before he took the big jump he wanted to talk to his children about it.

His friend said that if he had to make some calls, then he could use his phone. At first Greg couldn't get any of the numbers right. He was dialing people all over the country, but unfortunately none of those who answered were Hemingways. Using directory assistance he finally managed to get in touch with my brother Pat, who told him that he was sure the million dollars my father had in his Coconut Grove account was more than enough to survive on.

Whether Greg, once he'd come down off his manic high, would have actually gone through with his plans to divorce Ida and to help his children is another question. Still, the intent to change his life was certainly there. Like Ernest, he realized that a caretaker wife doesn't always act in her husband's best interests. Ida, as far as Greg was concerned, was in it for the money and always had been. She put up with Greg's extravagant behavior because as his wife, she was included in his estate. Mary Welsh endured the difficult last period of Ernest's life for similar reasons. Papa may have drank heavily, been verbally abusive to her, and groped every woman within arm's reach, but Mary knew that once he was gone, she would be in charge. She would be the one to organize his letters and posthumous novels, and eventually get to put in her own two bits with her memoir, *How It Was*. That would be her reward, and when she'd had enough of his depression and threats to kill himself, she cleared the path to his suicide by leaving the keys to his gun rack where she was sure he could get them.

About a week before the end of the month, my father went to a party at a friend's house in the Grove. Perhaps still feeling enthusiastic after his last conversation with my brother, and more than ever convinced of his decision to ditch Ida, he showed up dressed as a woman in a long black evening gown, with black high heels and a blond wig. Many of the people at the party remarked that he was in excellent spirits as he danced, joked, and drank his way into the early hours of the morning. His alias for the evening was not the usual Gloria, but instead, he used "Vanessa," his youngest daughter's name. He was feeling good about himself, and said to one person there that having his sex-change surgery was the best thing he'd ever done.

At around four a.m. he said good-bye to his host and started walking toward Key Biscayne. Moving down Bayshore Drive and Miami Avenue, he went past the aquarium turnstile at the entrance to the Rickenbacker Causeway. When I was a boy, the turnstile had a spinning replica of an enormous tiger shark that they'd caught out in the bay, and every time I'd go by it with my father in the car, or on the back of his motorcycle I'd look at it and think that it was good it was up there and no longer in the water. The turnstile still exists, but they got rid of the shark and replaced it with a group of frolicking dolphins. That morning my father would have seen the dolphins and not the shark as he strode by in his evening gown, an image certainly more in keeping with his manic high than a twelve-foot predator would have been.

Somewhere along the road, perhaps after he'd walked over the big bridge to Virginia Key, he decided to take off his dress and carry it. At that point the only thing he had on was his underwear, but even that had to go in his march across the island. Feeling un-inhibited was a recurring theme in Greg's manic phases. On a high, he would start to feel good about himself and his body, and whether it was walking into a cowboy bar in Montana in drag or stripping down naked and then standing up on a table in an ex-pensive Parisian restaurant, the message was always the same: *Look at me.* At the same time it was a way of provoking people, of rousing them out of their apathy and daring anyone to stop him. Most of the drivers who saw him probably didn't think much of the elderly, somewhat overweight, exhibitionist wandering past the Seaquarium. Miami was full of strange sights at night, and Greg was just one of the many.

Eventually the partying and the booze caught up with him, and he fell asleep on the beach at Crandon Park. He was out for about six hours, and when he awoke the sun was high overhead and his skin had started to turn red. He went back to the road and was walking down the median when Key Biscayne police officer Nelly Diaz spotted him and slowed down to have a closer look. My father saw the patrol car coming, and the first thing he did was to try to get his flowered underwear back on.

Unable to get his feet in through the leg openings of his panties, he decided to just forget about it and introduce himself to Officer Diaz. She asked him where he was going, and he said down to the lighthouse and back, and that some friends had just given him a lift from Miami. She noticed the sunburn on his face and chest and thought that apart from the fact that it was illegal to walk through the middle of Key Biscayne naked, and that she'd have to arrest him, it was also fairly obvious that he needed help.

On the way over to the station in the patrol car, Greg was talkative and charming as only my father could be. When he found out that she was Cuban, he said that he'd been on the island and that he liked the port of Mariel. Mostly, though, he talked about Africa and his hunting, how he didn't like the poachers, and how he'd nearly killed one once with his bare hands. He also said that he loved his father, but that it was difficult being his son and a transsexual at the same time. It didn't fit the image that people had of Ernest Hemingway. Nelly told Greg that she could understand his feelings, because she lived with a woman, and a lot of people resented that and didn't think it was right.

He told her that everyone should be accepted for who they were, and she said that it was ironic. She'd always been such a big fan of Ernest Hemingway, and now here she was talking to his son. My father thought that was cute, and promised her that when they let him out, he was going to look her up and take her out for lunch. "Anytime," she told him, and when they got to the police station, she had him sign his autograph on the back of the arrest affidavit. He wrote: "to the loveliest police officer i have ever met—greg hemingway."

They didn't keep him in Key Biscayne long. He barely had enough time to get dressed before he was transferred to the Miami-Dade County Women's Correctional Facility, where he was booked and his bond set at $1,000. Of course, that didn't mean that he had to pay a thousand dollars to get out. To post bail for an inmate, you only needed ten percent of the bond, which in my dad's case would have been a $100! Even I could have afforded that, and within an hour or two of calling a bondsman, Greg would have been on his way back to the Grove. In retrospect, it was a ridiculously low sum for someone like my father who had millions in his account, or for the absentee wife who was in control of his finances.

As a prisoner, there was no limit to the number of people Greg could contact, and while I don't know if he took advantage of this right, I'm certain that his wife knew where he was by the beginning of his second day in jail. Ida later stated in a newspaper interview that she was constantly trying to get in touch with the jail, and that she did her best to get her husband the medication he needed, but that the lines were always busy. However, when I toured the jail in April of 2005 and asked the director if it was that difficult to get through, she told me that calling them was the easiest thing in the world. There was always someone downstairs at the reception desk, ready to pick up the phone twenty-four hours a day, seven days a week. Also, Greg wouldn't have been able to receive any prescription drugs from his wife; that was something they didn't allow. But a family physician could have easily told them what my father was taking and this information would have then been referred to the jail's medical staff.

Ida's main excuse for not posting bail was that she wanted Greg to get professional help, and that if they'd let him go, then he would have been on the streets again without any kind of supervision. But if this was how she felt, and if she really did care for my father, then why wasn't she down in Miami doing everything in her power to have him released? After I finished talking to the director and was on my way out, I remember one of the guards telling me off the record that where he worked was not a hospital. "This is a jail, Mr. Hemingway, and we do what we can to help a prisoner. But you can't expect that someone like your dad is going to get the treatment here that he could get on the outside. We just aren't set up for that."

In fact, only if Ida had left Montana and flown down to Miami to be at my father's side could Greg have ever hoped to be treated as he should have been. Ida was the only one in the family who knew where he was, and if she'd gone to see a judge, she could have easily obtained a court order to have him released under the care of a psychiatrist. Legally speaking, it was more than doable. He could have been out in a day or two (at home and not wandering in the streets), and if he was taking his Lithium, finally on his way toward a full recovery. Instead, his wife ignored him. She did absolutely nothing, and Greg had no choice but to spend the five days that separated him from his arraignment locked up in a building that was claustrophobic in the extreme.

No one was sent to see my father, and no one called him. Ida had promised that he could rot in jail, and she seemed intent on keeping her word. Greg, for his part, didn't seem terribly upset about his predicament. He knew that eventually he'd get out, and he was biding his time. The director told me that he was calm inasmuch as a person in a manic phase *could* be calm, and that he liked to joke and talk. Many of the guards remembered him from the last time he'd been there in 1996.

On my tour of the jail in 2005, I was taken to the cafeteria where he'd eaten and the cell where he'd slept. Apparently a few months before my visit, the jail had had some problems with inmates coming down with infectious skin diseases, and there were signs everywhere reminding the women to wash their hands. The smell of industrial-strength Lysol on the floor was impressive, but it was the kind of place that you could never keep clean. The dirt was inherent in the setting itself. It accumulated under the coats of paint, on the steel beds, the porcelain toilets, and the metal sinks. It was an institutionalized filth, and when I asked the guard if I could be left alone in the cellblock, the sensation of drowning when he closed the door, of being entombed behind the reinforced walls, was something that I hadn't anticipated.

How could Ida have let this happen to Greg? How could she have let him stay here for as long as she did? She may have only been with him for his money, but this room was obscene, and I felt like pounding her face into the wall as I stood there. I had a desperate need to pin the blame on someone, but even if she did know and did nothing, not everything was her fault. It wasn't the first time that Greg had found himself behind bars, and what I should have asked myself was why he had continued to get himself arrested. This was but the last in a long line of incarcerations, and while there was probably little that anyone could have done to stop him from acting like a nut once he'd entered a manic phase, there was more to it here than just Greg dressing up or exposing himself for provocation's sake.

From the time of his mother's death, the first of October was a day that he could never ignore. "You killed her," Ernest had told him, and if as a physician my father later discovered that that wasn't true, I don't think he ever stopped blaming himself for what happened. In a manic phase, he'd acted irrationally, thinking only of himself, and had exposed his mother to the firing line of Ernest's wrath. With her type of cancer, just about anything could have triggered a fatal episode, but Greg always wondered . . . Had he acted differently, perhaps his mother wouldn't have died then—and especially under those circumstances. Had he behaved himself, she never would have phoned Ernest in Havana, nor would Ernest ever have been able to blame him, even though he couldn't control the obsessions or the manic outbursts. They were part of the disease, and no one really understood then what made him tick. It was the undiagnosed malaise, "the dark side," as my grandfather described it, or the family curse, as many journalists are fond of calling it. This was the source of Ernest's "black-ass periods," and the genetic link that he had with his son.

For many people my father was not exactly what you would call a Hemingway hero. His flamboyant, if somewhat confused, sexuality doesn't mix well with the stoic, tragic heroes of my grandfather's works. These were men who were always doomed from the start, their eventual defeat a given. But how they lived and endured the pain and inevitable death was the true test of their manhood. Did they courageously face their destiny, or did they stand down as cowards?

Looking back at my father's life, I don't know if I would have had his courage had I been born Ernest's son instead of his grandson. I've had my fair share of disappointments and problems, but nothing, I think, that can compare to what Greg went through. When people ask me if it's difficult having such a famous last name, I say that it hasn't been easy, but that I'm already one generation removed from my grandfather. I didn't grow up with the great writer. I wasn't his favorite son, or the boy who'd shown such promise and had inherited—along with the good looks and charming wit—all of the dark side that would eventually drive my grandfather to desperation and suicide. I didn't have to cope with that. Genetically I'd been dealt a different set of cards. I had a father who was bipolar, but a father who I realize now was stronger than most people would have given him credit for. In the end, he didn't kill himself and leave me with the feelings of inadequacy and blame that the children of suicides often feel. Taking seriously Ernest's words that "courage is grace under pressure," he avoided the "family exit." He faced his inevitable defeat, and when his heart went into fibrillation on the morning of October 1, 2001, fifty years to the day (almost to the hour) of his mother's death, there was no one there to see him on the floor as he struggled with his memories and sense of who he was.

He died alone, having endured the pain for as long as he could.

EPILOGUE

In Milan the summer humidity had already arrived, and on the 24th of May I took the bus to the hospital where Ornella had been for the last four days. She was in a room on the third floor of the maternity ward, and as I bounded up the stairs (I should have been there half an hour earlier) I thought that I would spend the time we had before noon, when visitors had to leave, chatting about work, the house, and the few letters that we'd received. Instead, I discovered that she'd gone into labor that morning and had been sent to another section on the second floor.

Immediately my heart started to pound. This was it, I thought. I raced down the stairs, and by the time I pressed the buzzer on the door to the delivery ward I was out of breath. In barely comprehensible Italian I asked the nurse where Ornella was. She told me that my wife was in the fourth room on the right, but that all visitors had to put on a green operating smock before going in.

I struggled with the sleeves of the smock, thinking that the damn thing was made to slow you down, but when I got to the door of her room, the sight of Ornella sitting calmly in her bed knocked me back to reality. Yes, she was in labor—the first contractions had started to come around five o'clock that morning—but she was still a long way from giving birth. In the beginning, the contractions came about once every hour, and now she was feeling the pain every half hour. I asked her how she was, and she said that they were getting stronger but nothing that she couldn't handle. I thought, well, if this was all there was to it, then having a baby was a breeze. Perhaps I'd seen too many Hollywood films with women screaming in brightly lit rooms, and the reality was altogether different.

I was wrong. The serious contractions started just before noon. Ornella called a nurse, who was finishing the night shift and who told us in a half yawn that everything was okay, that all was as it should be. "Il travaglio è così." (This is the way labor is.)

At one point, Ornella thought that if she got up and walked it might make the pain go away or, if nothing else, easier to deal with. So we started walking, but the contractions grew worse, coming every ten minutes. Ornella wasn't crying but she was close to reaching her limit. The pain would subside and then start again, and as I helped her along I wished that there was something more I could do. Finally, at around five o'clock in the afternoon, one of the nurses checked her and decided that Ornella was dilated enough and that it was time to move her to the delivery room.

There were no bright lights in the room, and everything was a lot smaller than I had imagined it would be. There was a stainless steel table with leg rests, but Ornella decided that she felt better standing, and that's how she gave birth to Michael. It was exactly six o'clock, and I remember that I cried when I saw my son. He was so beautiful, I thought, perfect in every detail. But almost as soon as he'd made his grand entrance, they took him to another room to clean him off and do their routine checks.

Epilogue

When they brought him back everyone left, Ornella included, and we were alone for a few minutes. I don't know if it consciously occurred to me, but with the birth of Michael, the psychological landscape of my family had changed. I had ceased to be just the son of Greg and had become a father myself. The shoe was really on the other foot now, and I couldn't very well go on complaining about what had or hadn't been done for me. I needed to think about Michael and what he needed. It was a tremendous responsibility, but at the same time (if I could see it for the gift that it was) an opportunity. The often-troubled father/son relationship that I had experienced with Greg, and Greg with Ernest, wouldn't necessarily have to repeat itself with my son. I could make amends and put a stop to the old pain. I couldn't forget where I'd come from, but I could understand and move on. That was all I wanted for Michael—a clean slate. As he looked up at me with the blue eyes that all newborns have, I told him, not to worry, that this time it'd be different. "I'll take care of everything, Mike, I promise."

Malaga, October 2006

ENDNOTES

1 Gerald Clarke, "The Sons Almost Rise," *Fame*, September 1989, page 108.

2 Kenneth S. Lynn, *Hemingway*, chapter 17, page 418.

3 Gregory H. Hemingway, MD, *Papa: A Personal Memoir*, page 20.

4 Kenneth S. Lynn, *Hemingway*, chapter 17, pages 418–419.

5 Bernice Kert, *The Hemingway Women*, chapter 3, page 247.

6 Gerald Clarke, "The Sons Almost Rise," *Fame*, September 1989, page 109.

7 John Colapinto, "The Good Son," *Rolling Stone*, September 2002, page 64.

8 Kenneth S. Lynn, *Hemingway*, chapter 22, page 533.

9 Ernest Hemingway, *The Garden of Eden*, 1986, page 14.

10 Ernest Hemingway, *The Garden of Eden*, 1986, page 15.

11 Ernest Hemingway, *The Garden of Eden*, 1986, page 17.

12 Mark Spilka, *Hemingway's Quarrel with Androgyny*, 1990, page 329.

13 Charles J. Nolan Jr., "Hemingway's Complicated 'Inquiry' in 'Men Without Women,'" *Studies in Short Fiction*, Vol. 32, 1995.

14 Nancy R. Comley and Robert Scholes, *Hemingway's Genders*, 1994, page 93.

15 Nancy R. Comley and Robert Scholes, *Hemingway's Genders*, 1994, pages 93–94.

16 Nancy R. Comley and Robert Scholes, *Hemingway's Genders*, 1994, page 94.

17 Nancy R. Comley and Robert Scholes, *Hemingway's Genders*, 1994, page 144.

18 Carl P. Eby, *Hemingway's Fetishism,* 1999, page 103.

19 Carl P. Eby, *Hemingway's Fetishism,* 1999, page 200.

20 Marcelline Hemingway Sanford, *At the Hemingways,* 1962, page 62.

21 Carl P. Eby, *Hemingway's Fetishism,* 1999, page 203, Letter to Mary, Copyright

   1998, Ernest Hemingway Foundation.

22 Gregory Hemingway, letter to Ernest, July 15, 1950.

23 Ernest Hemingway, letter to Gregory, December 14, 1950.

24 Russell Miller, *Bare-Faced Messiah,* edited by M. Joseph, 1987, chapter 10, page 174.

25 Russell Miller, *Bare-Faced Messiah,* edited by M. Joseph, 1987, chapter 10, page 166.

26 Gregory Hemingway, letter to Ernest, April 30, 1951.

27 Ernest Hemingway, cable to Gregory, April 30, 1951.

28 Gregory Hemingway, letter to Ernest, April 30, 1951.

29 Ernest Hemingway, letter to Gregory, May 2, 1951.

30 Gregory Hemingway, letter to Ernest, June 18, 1951.

31 Gregory Hemingway, *Papa: A Personal Memoir,* page 7.

32 Ernest Hemingway, letter to Gregory, February 22, 1952.

33 Gregory Hemingway, letter to Ernest, February 26, 1952.

34 Ernest Hemingway, letter to Gregory, March 2, 1952.

35 Ernest Hemingway, letter to Gregory, March 9, 1952.

36 Gregory Hemingway, *Papa: A Personal Memoir,* page 8.

37 Gregory Hemingway, letter to Ernest, July 3, 1952.

38 Gregory Hemingway, letter to Ernest, October 19, 1952.

39 Gregory Hemingway, letter to Ernest, November 3, 1952.

40 Gregory Hemingway, letter to Ernest, November 13, 1952.

41 Gregory Hemingway, letter to Ernest, November 14, 1952.

42 Ernest Hemingway, letter to Gregory, November 18, 1952.

43 Gregory Hemingway, letter to Ernest, November 21, 1952.

44 Gregory Hemingway, *Papa: A Personal Memoir,* pg. 9.

45 Gregory Hemingway, letter to Ernest, May 3, 1954.

46 Gregory Hemingway, letter to Ernest, July 16, 1954.

47 Gregory Hemingway, letter to Ernest, September 20, 1954.

48 Gregory Hemingway, letter to Ernest, October 6, 1954.

[49] Ernest Hemingway, letter to Gregory, October 12, 1954.

[50] Ernest Hemingway, letter to Gregory, October 12, 1954.

[51] Ernest Hemingway, letter to Gregory, October 13, 1954.

[52] Gregory Hemingway, letter to Ernest, October 25, 1954.

[53] Gregory Hemingway, letter to Ernest, August 20, 1957.

[54] Ernest Hemingway, letter to Gregory, August 24, 1957.

[55] Ernest Hemingway, letter to Gregory, January 20, 1958.

[56] Gregory Hemingway, letter to Ernest, January 29, 1958.

[57] Ernest Hemingway, letter to Gregory, February 4, 1958.

[58] Ernest Hemingway, letter to Gregory, February 7, 1958.

[59] Ernest Hemingway, letter to Gregory, May 1, 1958.

[60] Gregory Hemingway, letter to Ernest, January 27, 1961.

[61] Gregory Hemingway, letter to son John, August 19, 1985.